GRAND TIPS
for Bringing up Kids

Dudley Jones

Illustrations by
Philip Waddell

Positive Parenting Press

Positive Parenting Press
Reading
RG5 4NB
www.positiveparentingpress.co.uk

Copyright © Dudley Jones 2013

All rights reserved. No part of this book may be reproduced, adapted, stored in a retrieval system or transmitted by any means, electronic, mechanical, photocopying, or otherwise without the prior written permission of the author.

A CIP record for this book is available from the British Library

ISBN 978-0-9575303-0-0

Printed in the UK by Imprint Digital
Upton Pyne, Devon EX5 5HY

Typeset by: David English

About the Author

The author has spent most of his working life in teaching – in primary schools, secondary schools, and in teacher education at the University of Reading. He recently retired 'to spend more time with the grandchildren.' He has published numerous articles on children's literature and popular fiction, co-authored a biography of Lew Hoad, a tennis star of the 1950s and 60s, and co-edited a book: *A Necessary Fantasy? The Heroic Figure in Children's Popular Culture.*

He is married, has 2 children and 3 grandchildren.

For Lisa, Matthew, Charlotte, Connie, and Alex.

Contents

Introduction	6
Chapter 1: Three Golden Rules for Grandparents	8
Chapter 2: Coping with Mishaps, Tears, and Tantrums	11
Chapter 3: Rhymes, Picture Books and Stories for young Children	22
Chapter 4: Choosing Toys: Traditional v. Technological	38
Chapter 5: The Perfect Babysitter? Apps, TV, and DVDs	43
Chapter 6: 'Are we nearly there yet?'	55
Chapter 7: 'Food, glorious food!'	59
Chapter 8: 'Come on-a my house': Looking after Grandchildren in *your* Home	66
Chapter 9: 'Are you our *real* grandparents?'	70
Conclusion: Things a good Grandparent should never forget	75
Some activity rhymes to enjoy with your grandchildren	82
Children's picture books and poetry anthologies: an annotated reading list	86

Introduction

'Dad, what makes you think you're qualified to write a book on bringing up kids?'

'Well, my little Chickadee, I have spent nearly all my working life in education.'

'Yes, but... that was teaching at the Uni up the road, not engaging with real kids.'

'So the first five years teaching in schools, and the next thirty odd years regularly going into primary schools, doing workshops with kids... that's not engaging with real kids?'

'Yes, but-'

'And haven't I always spread sweetness and light and harmony amongst my grandchildren, turning their tears into laughter?'

'Yes, but-'

'And didn't your mother and I do a pretty good job of bringing up our own kids to be fine, upstanding members of the community?'

'Oh, yes. Obviously...'

'I rest my case.'

'Does this mean I have to pay for my copy?'

'Um... I might give you a small discount.'

I sometimes think my daughter would have got a good job with the Spanish Inquisition, but she was right to question my credentials. And since I escaped the rack and thumbscrew, I assume she was satisfied with my answers.

This book is intended not just for GRANDPARENTS but also for PARENTS – in fact, anyone who looks after kids on an occasional or regular basis. Although you won't find any psychological gobbledygook here, I do believe psychological approaches can be helpful in caring for kids. Not the kind of academic textbook psychology that blinds you with science, just common sense psychology expressed in everyday language.

You *will* find plenty of practical ideas for making the experience of looking after kids relaxing (let's face it: once you're past a certain age, it's sometimes a question of survival!) and also more rewarding and enjoyable for you – and them. I've restricted my focus to children up to the age of 7 which equates to pre-school, and Key Stage 1 of the primary school curriculum because these are the years in which most grandparents make a major contribution to childcare.

The book is arranged in sections dealing with topics like: 'Coping with mishaps, tears and tantrums', 'Choosing toys', 'and 'Storytelling'. As you can see from the (almost verbatim) conversation with my daughter above, much of the advice is based on being a parent and a grandparent. However, I'll also draw upon my experience as a teacher, lecturer and writer on children's literature and popular culture.

As a grandparent you have to re-learn some of those lessons you learnt long ago. But there are bonuses: you're still emotionally involved (of course) but there's a greater distance between you and the child; you can stand back, be more objective, and learn from the mistakes you made first time round. I remember a TV interview with the Archbishop of Canterbury many years ago. On the grand piano behind him was a printed card which said: 'If you learn by your mistakes... I'm getting a great education'. You could hardly get a better summing up of the educational/learning experience: advice that's admirably short and very consoling.

'Grandad's tips'? It should really be 'Grandad's and Grandma's tips' because I've relied so often on my wife's collaboration - both in life and in producing this book.

CHAPTER 1

Three Golden Rules for Grandparents

'Dad, you're so good with the kids. Would you like to look after them full-time?'

1. 'Make 'em laugh, make 'em laugh...'

Laughter is the best therapy. A recent study revealed that people who smile and laugh a lot are less prone to depression, and live longer. Hardly surprising, is it? You hate seeing children upset or crying? The quickest solution is to distract them, and better still, make them laugh. Laughter is a great way of defusing anger and tension. The phenomenal success of Roald Dahl demonstrates that children the world over love to be amused. Dahl's humour also appeals to grown-ups - which is why they'd sooner read his books to kids than Enid Blyton's. I want to see my grandchildren - all children – happy. It's difficult to laugh and be miserable at the same time: it's not impossible, just rare.

2. 'NO means NO!

Yes, I know this makes me sound like a tyrannical, authoritarian figure from a Dickensian novel but it is very important. You need some kind of command that secures instant obedience – no 'ifs' or 'buts'. Most children are disobedient at times, some more frequently than others. That's O.K. up to a point. There are plenty of situations where you can be flexible, where there's room for negotiation. Occasionally, though, situations arise where the child's safety, or the safety of others, is endangered and that's when instant obedience is imperative. One such situation would be when a child is approaching a busy road and is just beyond your reach (I realise in an ideal world this would never happen). You need a command that will instantly be obeyed.

Count how many times you say 'No' during a single day and – especially if there's more than one child - you'll be surprised how often it happens. I'm going to stick my neck out and suggest this applies to even the most liberal parent/grandparent. So what do you do? How do you get the child to distinguish between one kind of 'No' and another? That one 'No' has a greater force than another.

Sadly, I have no easy answer. If I had some magic solution that could be peddled to every schoolteacher with class control problems, I'd be a millionaire. Pamela Druckerman in *French Children Don't Throw Food* has a nice anecdote about the way French parents ensure their 'Non' is obeyed.

Druckerman, an American, moved to Paris to be with her French husband. She's out in the park with her two-year-old son, Leon, and her neighbour Frédérique. Her conversation with Frédérique is constantly interrupted because Leon keeps dashing outside the fence surrounding the play area. Each time she chases him, scolds him and drags him back while he screams. When Frédérique tactfully points out that this ritual makes conversation impossible, she says, 'That's true ... but what else can I do?', Frédérique smiles, urges her to be more firm, and tell Leon he mustn't leave the play area – and that this must be said with conviction. After four attempts, bolstered by her neighbour's encouragement, she achieves success.

Whether you raise your voice or adopt a particular tone, you have to be obeyed, and you have to find ways (a stern look, a furrowed brow?) of making it clear to children that your command cannot be questioned. And don't forget Frédérique's advice that whatever you say has to be said with conviction. If *you* don't believe it's going to happen, neither will your grandchild.

As far as dangerous situations are concerned (a child approaching a busy road say, or hitting other children) you may need to establish an alternative command like 'STOP!' This at least frees up 'No' for less serious occasions.

3. Avoid saying...

i 'Er, I don't think so' in response to 'Can we do x or y or z?' (when what you really mean is 'No'). Kids have a built-in radar device: the merest chink of light in your defence, and they'll drive a coach and horses through it.

ii 'Would you like to do x or y?' if you really want them to do x! Offer options only if you genuinely don't mind which one they choose. Otherwise, sure as eggs is eggs, they'll choose the one you don't want.

iii 'I don't know if you're going to like/enjoy this'. This is a real 'No-No'. It's the kind of thing you blurt out nervously when you've prepared some new culinary delicacy for them. Be a good salesman/woman – sell your product. If, for example, you have prepared a new dish, say, 'Now you're really going to enjoy this. It's the King and Queen's favourite dish!' I don't guarantee it will always work, but it stands a much better chance than the 'I don't know if...' opening gambit.

CHAPTER 2

Coping with Mishaps, Tears, and Tantrums

'What's that up in the sky? Can you see it? It's a flying elephant.' (p15)

'Take no notice of Grandad, Sis. He's totally bonkers.'

Cynically, I decided to make this one of the early chapters because, if you're browsing through this book in a bookshop, it's the kind of heading that might persuade you to buy it!

Mishaps

I wouldn't categorise minor falls, bruises, and grazes as accidents. Accidents are more serious. When a child has an accident you try to comfort them with love and sympathy, to reassure them, and you respond according to the severity of the accident. It may mean applying soothing ointment or TCP, bandaging a wound, or taking the child to the doctor.

But what to do if a child bumps into a table or falls over and has - at worst – a bruise or slight graze? These are what I'd call mishaps, and I've found an instant cure for the tears that inevitably ensue. Parenting and teaching have convinced me of the value of play and dramatisation, and my basic approach to mishaps (and tears and tantrums) is to turn minor misfortunes into a game and employ drama techniques to distract and/or get the child laughing. Of course, before responding in this light-hearted way, you must first check the injury to make sure it's a mishap, and not a more serious injury.

Imagine a situation where a child's fallen over and bruised their knee. You realise it's a very minor injury. 'Oh, dear', you say with genuine concern. You kneel down and, though it's obvious where the graze or bruise is, you fire a series of questions:

'Where does it hurt? Is it your foot?' [point to each part of the body as you ask these questions]

'No? Well is it your ankle?'

'It's not? Oh, yes, it must be your shoulder?'

'No? [employ tones of increasing surprise!] Ah, of course! It's your hand.'

It may not be necessary to cover the whole body but be sure to avoid the relevant part – until, **maybe**, the last question. Also bear in mind that a degree of over-acting may help! [If it's a graze, that doesn't preclude you applying TCP or an antiseptic cream]

So how do kids react to this? To begin with, their usual response is a mixture of anger and frustration. How can a grown-up be this stupid? By this time, they've invariably stopped crying. Well, they've had to answer all these questions; you can't pay attention to questions and concentrate on crying.

Soon the frustration (they shout 'No, it's my X) gives way to giggles and laughter as they realise it's a game. Meantime they've completely forgotten what it was that was hurting!

This strategy has never let me down. Not with my own kids, not with my grandchildren, with friends' kids - or even complete strangers' kids (they usually watch in amazement as this madman questions their children). On one occasion I was taking a group of teacher training students into school to conduct a drama workshop with children. We attended the morning assembly and then, as the kids were filing out at the end, one stumbled and hurt himself. I went over and employed my questioning approach. A few minutes later, he was laughing and my street-cred with the watching students soared.

The magic ointment

Another strategy which never fails is the 'Magic Ointment'. Call on this for minor injuries: for example, the child's fallen over but there's only the slightest mark, bruise, or bump. Sit them down and say, 'Doctor X (your name) has just the thing for that – Magic Ointment!'

Make it into an Oscar-winning performance: 'This magic ointment magically cures anything.' Then you open a door of an imaginary medicine cabinet (make a creaking noise). Laboriously remove the lid from a jar you've taken from the cupboard. Put your finger in and very gently apply the ointment to the injured spot. Embellish your performance in any way you wish: 'You can't see any jar/ointment? Well, of course not – it's magic... invisible! That's what makes it so special. It always works for me ... and grandma/mummy/daddy' etc.

Almost instantly (because it's magic) the ointment takes effect. I think young kids know it's only make-believe, a game, but they want to believe and join in the 'game'. Call it a placebo if you like but it's one that always works. I think you'll soon find whenever kids sustain these trivial injuries they'll start requesting 'Magic Ointment' – in fact, it may help you assess the seriousness of the injury. If they don't request it or respond eagerly to your offer, it probably isn't trivial. The other day, my 2 year-old grandson had a fall. 'Do you want some magic ointment?' I said. 'Yes', he replied and before I could make a move, he started mimicking my act with the creaky cabinet and jar.

There are always alternatives to the magic ointment. Recently I took my grand-daughter to the park and she fell off a roundabout in the playground area. Though she was upset, I could tell immediately she hadn't really hurt herself – she was just a bit shaken up. Once again, laughter came to my rescue. 'Well I fell off the climbing frame over there, Lottie, and I've lost my hand – look no hand.' Of course, I'd pulled my sleeve over my hand. For a moment she was intrigued and examined my sleeve closely. Then she realised what I'd done and burst out laughing.

Tears and tantrums

Why do children cry?

- They've really hurt themselves. O.K., many adults would cry – except there's this powerful taboo: to cry is unmanly (unless you're an *X Factor* contestant). So we bite our lip and repress the tears. Basically, though, we're just the same: tears are an understandable and justified response whether you're a child or an adult.

- They're emotionally upset. There can be a variety of causes: perhaps they have been separated from Mummy or Daddy (and don't realise this is only temporary). Adults are just the same: lovers/partners saying goodbye at train stations often give way to tears. It could be a child has lost a comfort blanket/doll just before bedtime. Is there an adult who can't identify with this situation, who doesn't feel acutely the child's distress? Because, of course, we can relate to it. To lose – or think we have lost - a trinket with a special emotional significance can be as distressing for us as the loss of the comfort blanket for the child.

- They haven't hurt themselves but they have a pain/are suffering discomfort/have a wet nappy or a temperature etc. As with the other causes of crying above, you provide sympathy and act accordingly.

So where is all this leading? I simply want to distinguish between crying that's an understandable and justified response to the situation (and therefore requires a sympathetic, comforting response) and crying where there's nothing much wrong. Don't underestimate the latter; this crying can wear down a tired carer almost as much as the other kind. Once again, you must assess the cause of the crying; often the 'not very much wrong' crying will sound slightly different – though I'd be hard pushed to define the difference. You just know when you hear it, it's a sort of instinctive thing.

Sometimes it's difficult to escape the feeling that crying is a default mode for young kids (I know I'm sticking my neck out here, and child psychologists will probably be dancing up and down with rage).

How should you respond – especially if there doesn't really seem to be anything fundamentally wrong with them? Clinical psychologist and child therapist, Dr Tanya Byron, suggests it's very difficult to reason with young children, especially when they're upset. Instinctively you want to sit them down and explain why allowing them to do X or Y would cause them more pain/be unfair on a sibling etc and in an ideal world this would be my preferred course of action. But kids, as Byron points out, don't have those powers of reasoning.

On the other hand I'm not saying you should ignore crying – whether it's the 'serious' kind, or the 'not very much to worry about' kind. It's just that parents or grandparents tend to immediately pile in with solicitous concern when nothing much is wrong. Sometimes excessive concern can be unproductive: crying brings attention, and sympathy is often followed up by consoling treats and sweets. Is this the message you want to send?

Crying is often caused by something trivial. It could be a case of a child objecting to a sibling borrowing (for a short period of time) a crayon. The more siblings there are, the more likely will be these minor squabbles, and sibling jealousy is a source of endless fights and tears.

There are also the unreasonable requests. I remember my daughter wanting a doll or a toy from a local shop on a Sunday (this was before Sunday opening was a regular occurrence). No amount of reasoning would placate her, or stem the flow of tears, and at that stage I was too inexperienced a parent to think of alternative solutions. Having now (re)encountered all these problems with grandchildren, I've adopted a different strategy: distraction techniques.

Distraction techniques

Crying! How to restore peace and calm for both child and carer? Answer: Think of some way to distract them:

'Oh, dear – what's that on the end of your nose? Can't you see it?' (strenuous attempt on their part to see end of nose). 'It wasn't there before was it?' Next it could be 'What's that on your tee shirt?' (it may have some design or emblem which the child can be cajoled into telling you about)

Or

'What's that up in the sky, Alex? Can you see it? It's a flying elephant, a green one. You don't often see that, do you? Oh, look – it's just disappeared behind that tree.' Continue to ring the changes on this. Flying pink elephants/sheep/pigs/ducks can lead into 'What noise does the duck/pig/etc make?' After a time, such ploys will have exhausted their shelf life and you'll have to come up with something different. Once the crying has stopped, try to focus their attention on something real, not imaginary.

The simplest things can distract young children. I still remember – all too vividly – when my daughter, aged 20 months, broke her leg. She was in a hospital bed, her leg in a plaster cast hoist on a pulley above her head. Every 90 seconds or so, she'd have a muscle spasm. It was agonising to watch. Although nothing could really cut through the pain she felt, we played the simple game most parents are familiar with: 'Show me a sad face/a happy face/a puzzled face/an angry face etc, etc.'

Then maybe we'd move on to 'What noise does the duck/cow/sheep/pig make?' I like to think these games provided a brief respite from the pain.

'No, don't laugh!'
Mentioning happy face/angry face reminds me of a little ploy you can adopt when a child's having a 'strop'. They're peeved because they haven't got their own way (despite all your attempts to explain why). They start to sulk. You get the Churchillian, downward-curling lower lip and the glowering-under-furrowed brow. Oh **NO**, trouble ahead, you think, and seek some way of clearing the air, of restoring peace and harmony.

'Show me a happy face', you cajole. The glowering intensifies (if looks could kill!). You try again – with the same result. Now switch to 'Show me an angry face' and, of course, they show the same expression.

'Very good!' you respond, with exaggerated enthusiasm. 'Can you do that again – only this time, make it even angrier ... Yes, that's excellent!' Repeat 2 or 3 times, and - if you don't get a smile or a laugh – try the following: 'Now, look, I **don't** want to see you laughing or smiling. No, please **don't** do it. No laughing, no smiling.' Again, a degree of over-acting is helpful here. My grand-daughter – now 5 - is familiar with this ploy and sometimes (with a mischievous look) plays it back to me and, when I'm using it on her 3 year-old brother, she'll even intervene and order him not to laugh.

All it might need to get the desired effect is for you to simulate 'corpse-ing' (a theatrical term where comedians pretend to collapse into giggles because what their partner's saying is so funny). Practise it a few times - I don't have to pretend very hard: I'm usually so close to genuine laughter. I've lost count of the number of times I've used this ploy with children/grandchildren, and it's rarely failed.

Needless to say, when you come together in smiles and laughter, it's a truly rewarding feeling.

When two or more kids get together they often become over-excited. They start racing around, shouting, laughing hysterically, and you know it won't be long before there's either an accident, or a quarrel develops. A handy tip: play the game of 'Statues'. '

Statues

As soon as I say 'freeze!' you have to stop and not move – become a statue.' As long as they haven't become too 'hyper', they'll respond to the game, and the concentration required makes them calm down. This can lead in to the 'slowmo' activity where the command 'slowmo' must be followed by slow motion (as in a film) movements. This requires even greater concentration and buys you a few precious moments of silence!

Never play one sibling off against another; I know, obvious. My wife warned me and I didn't listen. As soon as I tried it, I realised she was right. On the other hand, I doubt whether singling out one child who is standing perfectly still, or performing slow-motion movements skilfully, will lead to any damaged psyches!

Tantrams and 'the Terrible Twos'

You're probably familiar with the 'Terrible Twos' phenomenon. You're out with your two-year-old grandchild and maybe he or she starts to climb over the Christmas display in a local store or asks (O.K. summarily orders) you to purchase a toy. Either you try to reason with the child ('I forgot to bring my credit card with me' etc) or you try to prevent the wanton destruction of the Nativity scene that's reducing nearby toddlers to tears. Your grandchild goes into meltdown, terrifying not just you but everyone around you. Suddenly you've become the centre of attention. You hear whispers: 'Why can't he control that child?'

It's like one of those horror movies. Should you summon a priest to perform an impromptu exorcism? Welcome to the 'Terrible Twos'.

If you've never heard the phrase, don't worry; I don't recall people talking about the Terrible Twos when my children were toddlers. And the behavioural problems associated with this phase of a child's development (hitting, scratching, biting, screaming, etc) are not always confined to the second year. They can begin at 18 months and continue beyond the age of three. Then you might encounter a phenomenon that some have labelled the 'Troublesome Threes'! At least 'troublesome' sounds lower on the emotional Richter scale than 'terrible'.

The Causes of temper tantrums

As every teacher knows, before you can do anything about disruptive behaviour, you need to discover what causes it. To begin with, a toddler's view of the world is a very egocentric one. Young children believe the world revolves around them and they find the concept of sharing difficult – don't expect the egalitarian principle of 'all for one and one for all' to spontaneously blossom. Fights inevitably break out over the possession of toys, for example, as you struggle to instil notions of turn-taking. Don't despair: they do learn to share - it just takes a little time.

There are other sources of frustration that lead to tantrums. Toddlers want to exert control, to push the boundaries of what grown-ups will accept (or tolerate). It's as if they're testing you: 'Go on, so I've made mud pies on the new carpet. What you going to do about it?' The thing is, whilst little kids don't have the ability to reason and are not susceptible to logical argument, they do seem to know instinctively what buttons to push, and exactly how far they can test your patience before World War Three breaks out.

So what do you do? Well, take a deep breath, count to ten. It's just possible they thought the new carpet was the ideal location for making mud pies. On the other hand, you don't want to establish a worrying precedent. Tell them calmly (but with hard stare) that it's wrong and it's a 'time out' session on the (naughty) step. I know the 'step' always feels like an admission of failure but it's the only non-violent intervention that seems to work. Two or three minutes are probably enough, followed up by a bit of affectionate bonding.

Other problems may occur because toddlers are frustrated by their linguistic limitations. They are beginning to acquire a vocabulary and, as they grow older, they understand how to construct simple (not always grammatically correct) sentences. I remember thinking a great future beckoned for my three-year-old son when he asked, 'Whobody buyed that, Daddy?' It may not have been a perfectly correct sentence but he'd demonstrated an understanding of fundamental linguistic principles. You formed certain pronouns with a prefix plus the suffix 'body' – thus 'nobody', 'somebody', 'anybody' and 'everybody'. What could be more natural – and logical – than 'whobody'? Similarly he'd realised the past tense of a verb is often formed by adding 'ed' and came up with 'buyed'.

When the child tries to express ideas or feelings just beyond their linguistic grasp, however, they can become very upset and frustrated. Sometimes this results in stammering. The stammer will often disappear as the child's language abilities develop. Creating a calm environment for children can also help to overcome the stammer and the aggressive responses it provokes. Remember, though, that stammering may have other causes and it's best to seek professional advice.

What generally worries parents and grandparents more than anything else are tantrums that lead to violent behaviour like hitting, scratching or biting. Clearly other children's safety is paramount but try not to overreact. Excluding your grandchild from situations like toddler groups or playing with friends leads to isolation and unhappiness, and doesn't really address the problem. Ultimately, of course, exclusion – even if it's temporary – may represent the only solution. Certainly, if there's a risk of injury, **you have to intervene quickly**. Tanya Byron suggests adopting a calm and assertive approach with a two-minute spell in another room. I have tried this and it worked – though it required quite a bit longer than two minutes! I was careful to fold my arms round the child (which served to protect me from kicking and scratching) and wait until the storm subsided. Byron concludes:

> Any intervention must involve no communication *[I'm not sure mine did]* and once the two minutes are up a brief explanation is in order: "If you bite again you will go in that room or face the wall."
>
> Nice behaviour is then praised and the child cuddled so he or she quickly learns which behaviours are rewarding and must continue, and which should stop because they get him or her no attention at all. [The Times 12th December 2011, T2 p9]

Temper tantrums may be, as Byron suggests, an attention-seeking device. If the child is demanding something that's clearly unreasonable, then ignore him or her. If you automatically submit to the child's demands, you create a rod for your own back, and re-establishing your authority becomes incredibly difficult. Adults, fearing for the child's safety, tend to impose limits which they find frustrating and rebel against. But this desire for greater independence can be looked upon as a positive development. Toddlers want to do more and more for themselves; within safe surroundings, this is something to be encouraged.

It's not only their physical capabilities that are developing: they are beginning to flex their mental 'muscles'. There's a growing awareness that adults can be manipulated, either by tantrums or by more subtle methods. Where some boys (but not all) resort to anger and aggression to get what they want, girls often favour charm. The recognition that Grandad can be won over with a polite request (a double 'please') and a cute smile, seems to be wired into their DNA. Be warned: the charm offensive can be a very potent weapon!

If your child displays extreme forms of unruly behaviour, and these persist, it's just possible he or she may be suffering from Pathological Demand Avoidance Syndrome (PDA), a little known condition similar to autism. As Guilia Rhodes explained in a Times article, children with PDA share 'an unusual resistance to everyday demands – even when related to things that they would enjoy.' The condition affects boys and girls almost equally.

Many of the symptoms displayed by sufferers of PDA are, of course, typical of normal healthy children but with PDA they continue beyond toddler years. For most children, says Rhodes, 'the demand avoidance phase will pass, or can be greatly improved through strategies such as rewards and sanctions (sticker charts, time out or a naughty step), reasoning, praise for good behaviour, peer pressure, and routine. But these techniques do not work for children with PDA.' (The Times, December 17, 2011, T2, p6).

I don't want to alarm you; it is extremely unlikely your child suffers from PDA. If you have strong grounds for believing they do, you should seek professional advice. The good news is that treatment for the condition is usually effective.

I think it would be wrong to claim all toddlers go through this phase of temper tantrums – some seem to serenely sail through them, skilfully navigating those emotional storms. And for those who don't, I hope I've been able to shed light on the causes of tantrums and to suggest possible remedies.

CHAPTER 3

Rhymes, Picture Books and Stories for Young Children

A child's first experience of poetry will usually be a parent reciting nursery rhymes. Few things are more rewarding for child (and adult) than the shared enjoyment of this traditional form of oral poetry (bear in mind that most poetry is meant to be heard). In a memorable phrase, the poet Seamus Heaney described the enforced poetry of his childhood (the sprung rhythms of the old radio weather forecast, the chanting of the Catholic litany) as 'verbal music bedding the ear with a kind of linguistic hardcore that could be built upon some day'. Nursery rhymes are part of that verbal music, laying down the same poetic foundation.

The child first becomes aware of rhyme and rhythm – and song – through the music of nursery rhymes. The alliterative bounce of 'Half a pound of tuppenny rice/Half a pound of treacle/That's the way the money goes/Pop goes the weasel' exerts an hypnotic attraction, and kids always relish – and join in - the explosive, onomatopoeic 'Pop!' of the final line.

Many nursery rhymes were intended for an adult rather than a child audience, and date back to the 17th and 18th century. 'Pop goes the weasel', for example, is an 18th century rhyme that uses cockney rhyming slang. 'Weasel' was an abbreviation of 'weasel and stoat' (coat) and 'pop' was a word for 'pawn' so if you 'popped your weasel' you pawned your coat. Some nursery rhymes are widely believed to incorporate satirical commentaries on contemporary figures and political events (e.g. 'The Grand Old Duke of York').

Unaware of these associations, young children simply respond to the musicality and charm of nursery rhymes. These rhymes, however, aren't just a source of aural pleasure, they also play an important part in a baby's cognitive development. As Alison Davies points out in her book *Reading to your baby*, nursery rhymes 'have an ebb and flow that appeals to tiny ears, they are fun'. Parents and grandparents enjoy repeating them and, if you use them regularly, babies will 'retain information by learning sequences and patterns' (Davies, pp28-9).

There are several excellent collections of nursery rhymes; most are beautifully illustrated, but illustrations aren't really necessary – I suspect they are more for the enjoyment of grown-ups. One that I liked (and my grandchildren always requested) was *Ride a Cock-Horse* (Sarah Williams, illustrated by Ian Beck). The book's sub-title, *Knee-jogging rhymes and lullabies*, reminds us that nursery rhymes usually involve action. Apart from "Ride a Cock-Horse', 'Rub-a-Dub-Dub', and 'Rock-a-Bye-Baby', you won't find many of the best known nursery rhymes in Williams' book but there are some captivating ones I'd either forgotten, or never encountered. I especially enjoyed 'Dance to your Daddy' ('My bonnie laddie') and 'Down at the Station' which has lots of 'Chuff-chuff' sounds! [can these really be classified as nursery rhymes? I don't know and I don't care - they're such fun]

The book is divided into four sections: Knee-Jogging Rhymes; Bouncing and Dancing Rhymes; Patting and Clapping Rhymes; Lullabies and Rocking Rhymes. At the beginning of each, there are helpful suggestions for accompanying activities: Knee-Jogging rhymes, for example, where the baby rides on your knees or crossed legs, and the 'rate of jogging varies with the rhythm of the words, but usually starts quite gently and ends vigorously.' One of my grand-children's favourite activity rhymes (about horse-riding) employs similar movements:

Young ladies go nim, nim, nim *(child on your knees, lady-like movements up and down)*

Young gentlemen go clip-clop, clip-clop, clip-clop *(more vigorous movements)*

And old farmers go gallopy, gallopy – DOWN IN A DITCH! *(growing louder, faster, and then pause after 2nd 'gallopy' and finally, supporting child's head, lower them so they end up lying on top of your outstretched legs)*

I'm sure many of you are already familiar with a number of activity rhymes. If you're not, you'll find a selection at the end of this book.

Perhaps because the child in me is still alive and kicking, I still delight in playing 'Round and round the garden/Like a Teddy Bear/ One step, two steps/Tickley under there' [finger tickles tummy and ends up tickling the armpit] with my grandchildren. Or 'This little piggy went to market/This little piggy stayed at home/This little piggy had roast beef/This little piggy had none/And this little piggy went wee-wee-

wee, all the way home.' Here you start with the little toe and work your way across.

I'm sorry if all this sounds like I'm teaching Granny to suck eggs. The only reason I'm talking about these old favourites is because recently there have been reports of nursery rhymes dying out. Parents, we're told, are no longer reciting them to their children – they're not being handed down from one generation to the next. If this is really the case, it's worrying, but I suspect the demise of nursery rhymes has been greatly exaggerated.

Ride a Cock-Horse is currently out of print. However, copies are available on Amazon at a very modest price, and can be purchased with an accompanying CD. My copy came from a charity shop.

Another of my grand-children's favourite books is *One, Two, Flea* by Allan Ahlberg, illustrated by Colin McNaughton. Ahlberg and McNaughton are highly respected figures in the world of children's literature, and these nonsense rhymes with their zany illustrations are guaranteed to have grown-ups and kids giggling hysterically. The hypnotic refrain of 'Tiny Tim' cries out to be chanted, and takes me back once more to my own childhood:

In comes the doctor
In comes the nurse
In comes the lady
With the alligator purse

"Dead!" says the doctor.
"Dead!" says the nurse.
"Dead!" says the lady
With the alligator purse.

But she isn't!

The sensory pleasure I get from reciting the line, 'the lady with the alligator purse', is difficult to explain. And what does the alligator purse look like in McNaughton's picture? Well, like a pair of handles attached to an alligator, of course! [Again this book is out of print, but available online]

Most kids need no encouragement to start making up new versions of poems. My grandson recently surprised me by singing:

Twinkle, twinkle, chocolate bar,
My dad drives a rusty car.
Pull the lever, push the choke,
Off we go
In a cloud of smoke.

I assumed it was a rhyme he'd made up or picked up from other children in the playground. Later, I discovered *Twinkle, Twinkle, Chocolate Bar* was the title of a collection of poems by the children's poet, John Foster. This was embarrassing because I know John quite well!

I recall my 8 year-old daughter shyly reciting a verse that was circulating in the playground, and that she clearly thought was very daring:

Teacher, teacher, I declare,
I can see your underwear.
Is it black or is it white?
Oh my God, it's dynamite!

No doubt it's a rhyme that's still going the rounds. Iona and Peter Opie's wonderful book, *The Lore and Language of Schoolchildren* shows how playground rhymes reflect changing social and historical conditions. One that particularly fascinated me, obviously originates from the Second World War period:

When the war is over Hitler will be dead,
He hopes to go to heaven with a crown upon his head.
But the Lord said, No! You'll have to go below,
There's only room for Churchill, so cheery, cheery oh

A valuable online resource can be found by googling 'National Curriculum Phonics: rhythm and rhyme for young children'. This will bring up the relevant NC documents and if you scroll down to **Letters and Sounds: Phase One, Aspect 4: Rhythm and Rhyme** you will find some excellent suggestions for activities involving rhythm and rhyme. Here are a couple of examples:

Songs and rhymes

Include a selection of songs within the daily singing session which involve children in experimenting with their voices. Simple nursery rhymes such as 'Hickery, Dickery, Dock' provide an opportunity for children to join in with 'wheeee' as the mouse falls down. Use this to find related words that rhyme: dock, clock, tick-tock. Substitute alternative rhyming sounds to maintain children's interest and enjoyment.

Finish the rhyme

Use books with predictable rhymes that children are familiar with and then stop as you come to the final word in the rhyme. Invite children to complete it. Use plenty of intonation and expression as the story or rhyme is recounted.

These suggestions are intended for teachers but I see no reason why you shouldn't use them with your grandchild.

Reading aloud poems and stories

Remember that a performance of a rhyme (or story) usually benefits from a little rehearsal. You don't need a degree in Performing Arts but if you aren't used to reading aloud, a few tips may be helpful:

- If possible, get hold of one of those old tape recorders – or smart phone - and record yourself reading a story. If you're horrified when you play it back, don't despair: the poor quality of reproduction emphasises the treble notes, making your voice sound more 'tinny'.
- I bet the first 'technical' thing you'll notice is that you're going too fast. It's easy to slow down. Try reading at what seems a ridiculously slow pace; you'll probably end up somewhere in the middle and children will find it much easier to absorb what you're saying.
- There are lots of CDs and DVDs of accomplished performers reading stories. Try listening/watching them – you'll find it a very pleasurable experience, and also pick up a lot of useful tips. One of my favourite CDs is Maureen Lipmann reading Jill Tomlinson's *The Owl Who Was Afraid of the Dark.*
- If you're feeling adventurous, have a go at employing different voices for different characters. If that sounds daunting, you can just take a longer pause before a character starts speaking:' "I'll blow your house down!" [pause] he said'. In this way you're highlighting dialogue.
- There's a natural tendency for the voice to drop at the end of phrase or sentence (what Shakespeare called 'a dying fall'). It's not something we notice when we're talking to people but the regular sound pattern

can become a little monotonous when you're reading. Compensate by sometimes pushing your voice up at the end of lines. It'll sound artificial at first but you'll soon get the hang of it.

- Try to occasionally look up at your listener/s – make eye contact. Experienced readers can do this by scanning ahead but even if you're not an experienced reader, as long as you're familiar with the story, it's quite easy to find your place on the page again.

Above all, you must be interested in what you're reading. If you're not interested, or don't sound as if you are, it will quickly be communicated to the child.

Whilst I believe these performance tips can enhance the magic of stories and poems, ultimately they can only provide a little extra icing on the cake. The main thing is that you do actually read to children - there are few activities so valuable and mutually rewarding.

If you want more tips on ways of improving your reading aloud skills and bringing picture books and stories to life, I'd recommend Dee Reid's and Diana Bentley's excellent book *Helping your child to read* in Hodder Education's Teach Yourself series. They provide a sentence-by-sentence, picture-by-picture guide to reading aloud a famous picture book, *Mr Gumpy's Outing* by John Burningham (you may be familiar with another Burningham picture book, *Granpa* which was made into a Channel4 animated film).

Reid and Bentley also stress the importance of sharing books with children and, of course, talking to them! It not only helps to make their lives happy and fulfilled, they say, but also helps their language and reading development. They cite a study by Professor Barry Zuckerman of the Department of Pediatrics at Boston University School of Medicine who says that if you could imagine someone coming up with a widget that would stimulate all aspects of a two-year-old's development, that widget would be a book! (Zuckerman in Dee and Bentley p54)

Picture books and stories

You'll often want to share a picture book with your grandchildren. Sometimes they'll have a large selection, and will request a particular favourite. There'll be other occasions, however, when you'll enjoy choosing for them – from a library or bookshop. And it's nice being able to recommend titles for harassed parents.

What makes your choice easier is that during the last half century we've been enjoying a golden age of children's literature. Brilliant new illustrators and writers have created a dazzling variety of books for all ages, and tastes.

For the very young there are several different types of picture books:

- Some have small amounts of text; in others, the illustrations complement and enhance the text but the narrative is far more dependent on words. And there are even wordless picture books.

- Cloth books – remember the seductive appeal of these? The feel of them and being able to chew the pages ? Or books with thick card pages that stood up to the rough treatment of tiny hands. Your child wants a book in the bath? Yes - there are even soft plastic books for bath-time.

- Ingeniously designed Pop-up books have almost become a separate art form. Maybe they're best kept away from very young children because they're so easily damaged! Other interactive books simply invite the child to lift a flap, pull a lever, or take a letter from an envelope (e.g. *The Jolly Postman* by Janet and Allan Ahlberg).

- Books in the form of DVDs (e.g. Michael Rosen's *We're all going on a Bear Hunt*) or electronic books for an iPad.

Stories that help children deal with difficult issues

Reading (perhaps 'sharing' is a better word) a picture book, or a story, provides a marvellous opportunity to bond with the child: a shared experience in which you can discuss and ask questions about the story – and the pictures. It also enables you to confront and overcome common fears. I remember my 4 year-old daughter's fears of the dark were allayed by reading Jill Tomlinson's delightful story, *The Owl Who Was Afraid of the Dark*.

Death and bereavement are, of course, painful subjects that need to be handled with great sensitivity. Debi Gliori's *No Matter What*, is a picture-book that reassures young children about the unconditional nature of a parent's love: a 'grim and grumpy' little fox called Small repeatedly asks whether Large (his mother? – genders are never specified) will still love Small regardless of what he [oops!] does. Each time Large replies, 'I'll always love you no matter what.'

Finally, Small asks the question most adults dread: 'But what about when we're dead and gone, would you love me then, does love go on?' The reply suggests that love endures and transcends even death. Large points to the stars in the sky, some of which died a long time ago, and says, 'Still they shine in the evening skies, love like starlight never dies.' I can't think of a more sensitive and satisfying way of handling this basic human fear, and by the end of the story, I'm reaching for my box of Kleenex tissues.

Two other books that confront this most painful reality are John Burningham's *Granpa*, and Susan Varley's *Badger's Parting Gifts*. Burningham is a writer/illustrator who has enjoyed popular and critical acclaim. *Granpa*, like many of his picture books, has one side of a double page in predominantly pastel colours and sepia line drawings on the other. The text simply consists of dialogue – short snatches of conversation between Granpa and his grand-daughter which are mostly placed above the sepia drawing on the left. The one variation occurs in the centre pages where the delicately coloured picture fills the 2 pages. It shows Granpa seated in a garden chair, pretending to eat ice-cream from a flower pot that's clearly been given to him by his grand-daughter. She is surrounded by her toys and garden tools, against a backdrop of a greenhouse and garden shrubs. The caption above reads: 'This is lovely chocolate ice-cream.' (bold type) and *'it's not chocolate, it's strawberry.'* (italics). Granpa's comments are always in bold type, the little girl's in italics.

This double page perfectly captures the relationship between grandfather and grand-daughter -the former joining in the child's make-believe game, the girl innocently correcting him – and it demonstrates Burningham's mastery of the picture-book form.

On another occasion the girl asks, *'When we get to the beach can we stay for ever?'* and the reply comes, 'Yes, but we must get back for our tea at four o'clock.' Towards the end of the story, Granpa betrays signs of frailty. 'Granpa can't come out to play today' with Granpa in a chair, covered by a rug, medicine bottles on a table beside him. The next double page: Granpa, little girl on his lap and the caption, *Tomorrow, shall we go to Africa, and you can be the captain?* The penultimate pages have the little girl looking [across the page] at Granpa's empty chair. The last page is a brightly coloured picture of a girl pushing her toy pram up a hill.

If I've dwelt at length on this picture book, it's because it presents me with a problem. For me, it's a beautiful work of art: the most sensitive and moving depiction of the relationship between grandfather and grand-daughter. But there are times – especially towards the end – where it's unbearably poignant, and it always reduces me to tears (even when I'm reading it on my own!). Given my emotional reaction, how could I possibly contemplate reading/sharing it with children?

The problem, of course, lies partly in the unflinching honesty of Burningham's approach to death. While the final (caption-less) picture contains a hint of life renewing itself and the child overcoming her grief and sense of loss, there's no getting away from the bleak reality of the empty chair on the penultimate page. If you're made of sterner stuff than me and decide you'd like to read *Granpa* to your grandchild, I suggest you think very hard about the right time to introduce it.

Badger's Parting Gifts is a charming tale about a much-loved badger who's close to death. We're told he's 'not afraid of death'. After all, dying only means leaving his body behind, and since his body's not working too well these days, this doesn't concern him. He's only worried about his animal friends who will grieve for him. He tells them he'll shortly be 'going down the Long Tunnel'. He writes a letter, bidding them farewell. Naturally when his friends learn of his death they are very upset but, as the months pass, they often gather to remember gifts they'd received from Badger. Each animal has a special memory of Badger – 'something he had taught them that they could now do extremely well'.

Because *Badger's Parting Gifts* is about animals and not humans, it makes Badger's death easier for children to accept. Also, he's not afraid of death, indeed he almost welcomes it, and his friends are sustained by happy memories of the ways he's enriched their lives. Similarly, because *No Matter What* only touches on death and generally carries such an upbeat message, I'd have no qualms about reading that book at any time.

Finally, if your grandchild is sad about the death of a pet (something that happens all too frequently and affects adults as well as children) I can't think of a better book to cheer you up than Posy Simmond's *Fred*. Fred is a cat and, like *Badger's Parting Gifts*, the consolation comes in the form of a celebration of Fred's life by the local cats at his funeral. (further discussion of *Fred* can be found in the recommended reading list at the end of this book)

Stories in a multi-cultural community

It's important that picture books reflect the ethnic diversity of our multi-cultural community. As writer, teacher, and lecturer, Prue Goodwin, points out:

> All stories are valuable but for children the most valuable are often those stories from their own families, communities and cultures. The traditions of our cultural heritage conveyed through stories can be a strong part of our sense of identity, and, thus, our sense of self.
> [*Riveting Reads: Book Ahead: 0-7*, p9]

At the same time Goodwin recognises the value of children hearing stories about the world and its peoples. Stories are a form of knowledge, and children's understanding and awareness of other cultures will be enriched through the stories we share with them.

Fairy tales

One type of story that never seems to wane in popularity is the fairy tale. Critics argue about how to define fairy tales but I want to sidestep academic debates. For me, fairy tales involve:

- a clear distinction between good and evil (we have no difficulty distinguishing heroes and heroines from villains)

- magic – for example, a potion that makes someone sleep for a 100 years

- some kind of social and/or physical transformation (the humble peasant rescues the princess and marries her; the frog is changed into a prince after the princess kisses him)

Fairy tales sprang from the people; they were a folk art, orally transmitted, passed on from one generation to the next. In the 18th and 19th centuries, middle-class researchers, like Charles Perrault, and the Brothers Grimm, started transcribing, 'polishing', and publishing collections of these tales

Like nursery rhymes, fairy tales were originally intended for an adult audience. Because only wealthy people could afford books, the earthy and horrific details of many early versions of fairy tales had to be toned down or removed before they could be read to upper-class young ladies. 'Little Red Riding Hood', for example, contained sexual messages and scatological content that would scandalise a modern audience, let alone an 18th century one!

Regrettably, today we tend to read children those tales selected by Disney Studios for film adaptation. Disney classics from the 40s and 50s featured passive heroines dependent on a handsome prince to rescue them from wicked predators. The success of such films established the stereotype of the blue-eyed, blonde princess, an image reinforced by girls' clothing and doll manufacturers.

In the last 20 to 30 years, there's been a reaction against this stereotyping. You don't have to be a feminist to be concerned about the submissive role being held up for impressionable young girls. Stories like Babette Cole's *Princess Smartypants* (great title!) and Robert Munsch's *The Paper Bag Princess* began to appear. Wimpy girls were replaced by feisty, can-do heroines who didn't need men to rescue them from dungeons and dragons. *Princess Smartypants* and *The Paper Bag Princess*, reject the notion of marriage as their ultimate destiny. Smartypants keeps giant slugs as pets and challenges her princely suitors to roller-disco marathons. She kisses Prince Swashbuckle to turn him into a toad, and – unconcerned by her single status – 'lives happily ever after.' In *The Paper Bag Princess*, a dragon burns everything Princess Elizabeth owns, and carries off her beloved, Prince Ronald. She dons a paper bag, outwits the dragon and frees Ronald. Alas, the gallant prince is affronted by her paperbag outfit (and her smoky perfume). Wisely, Elizabeth decides he's not the man for her.

What prevents these and other 'progressive' tales from being preachy is their humour. Grown-ups and children love the witty reversal of traditional motifs. I have one minor reservation: much as I like a good laugh, this new breed of subversive fairy tales often excludes the mystery and the mixture of emotions (fear, pathos, and fulfilment) found in traditional tales like 'Hansel and Gretel' and 'The Snow Queen'.

The frightening nature of many fairy tales, however, has led to some parents/grandparents becoming concerned about the levels of violence in these stories and their potentially disturbing effect on children. The concern is understandable. Fairy tales address deep-seated childhood fears: being abandoned by parents; terrifying sibling jealousy and conflicts between children and step-parents (and *their* offspring); kidnapping, mutilation and hideously painful death; and - as if this gruesome catalogue was not enough - some of the tales in their original form involve sexual perversion and rape.

So why do most of us read fairy tales to children, take them to see film adaptations, and look back upon them with such affection? The answer is, of course, because we are only familiar with the sanitised versions of Disney. Even the Brothers Grimm toned down the more distressing elements of a tale like 'Hansel and Gretel', and later versions of 'Little Red Riding Hood' are almost unrecognisable from the original. Granted that the versions we know still contain moments that are genuinely shocking and disturbing, you might wonder at parents' and grandparents' willingness to expose children to such popular stories as 'Hansel and Gretel', Little Red Riding Hood', 'Rumplestiltskin' and 'The Little Mermaid'. I think it's because they allow children to play out their deepest fears in an environment that's safe: they listen to these stories with parents in a familiar setting. The story creates a magical secondary world and offers a comforting resolution, and if it gets too painful, too distressing, the primary world is always close at hand.

What adults tend to forget is that children (like us) enjoy being frightened! I remember my own children's response when they were about 6 and 8 years-old to 'Strange Visitor', a traditional ballad, and Disney's *Snow White and the Seven Dwarfs*. 'Strange Visitor' is a ghost poem. I had been encouraging students to read it to KS2 pupils in primary school, and I thought I'd try it out on my own children. I realised my son was a little young for such a scary poem but somehow sensed he would take it in his stride and enjoy it. The ballad begins with a woman sitting by her spinning wheel at night:

A wife was sitting at her reel ae night [ae=one]
And aye she sat, and aye she reeled, and aye she wished for company.

Her wish is soon granted for in comes a 'pair o' braid, braid soles' and sits down beside her, swiftly followed by a pair of small, small legs and then a pair of 'muckle, muckle hands' [muckle = large] and so on. Finally, a great big head sits down on a small, small neck.

The ballad is split into 2 halves. In the second half, there's a series of questions from the wife:

'Why hae ye such braid, braid feet?' quoth the wife
'Muckle ganging, muckle ganging' (gruffly)

'And why have you such small, small legs?'
'Aih-h-h!-late-and wee-e-e-moul' (whiningly)

'Muckle ganging' (I think!) means "much travelling." "Aih-h-h!-and wee-e-e-moul", I've always believed, is the wife mimicking the howling wind; it forms the second line of each couplet in the second half just as 'And aye she sat and aye she reeled' etc completes each couplet in the first. The poem concludes with the woman asking the ghost (who represents Death): 'What do you come for?'. Back comes the terrifying reply:

'FOR YOU!' (At the top of his voice, with a wave of the arms and a stamp of the feet)

The response of my children was fascinating. They sat on the sofa riveted, and leapt in the air at the deafening last line. Then immediately – and on succeeding nights – they wanted it read again.

But when it got to the penultimate line, they went and hid behind the sofa so they couldn't see me!

Their reaction to *Snow White and the Seven Dwarfs* was equally instructive. They were gripped by the Wicked Queen in the film's opening passage so the appearance of the 7 Dwarfs – amusing and charming – came as a welcome relief, releasing the tension. After a while, though, the charm wears thin; you could sense all the children in the cinema becoming restless, wanting something dramatic to happen. And then the Queen returns disguised as an old woman. She entices Snow White into taking a bite from her red, rosy apple. A frisson of fear ran through the audience, affecting children and adults alike.

It dawned on me: young and old enjoy being frightened, it seems to be hard-wired into our DNA. Just so long as we have that safety net of a familiar, cosy world to return to.

In the 1980s, dissatisfaction with traditional fairy tales fuelled a renewed interest in folk tales. Magic plays little or no part in these; instead, it is the heroine's or hero's cunning and resourcefulness that rescues them from danger. Writer and critic, Alison Lurie, argued that male editors and publishers had concentrated on folk tales and fairy tales that reinforced male dominance. Her collection *Clever Gretchen and Other Forgotten Fairy Tales* included 15 tales from various cultural and ethnic traditions about brave and intelligent girls. Similar collections of tales from India, China, and other parts of the world, soon followed.

A sub-genre of folk tales featured trickster figures; the trickster could be part animal, and part human, and children from the USA and the Caribbean enjoyed the amusing tales of Brer Rabbit and Anancy, a spider. Other cultures have generated their own trickster figures but Brer Rabbit and Anancy seem to travel well and will be familiar to many British children.

> It's beyond the scope of this book to provide a comprehensive, annotated list of fairy tale (and folk tale) collections, picture books, poetry and stories, but I can do the next best thing which is refer you to an excellent website: www.bookahead.org.uk. Here you can consult or download a booklet (68 pages), *Riveting Reads: Book Ahead 0-7 years*. At the back of this book you will also find a short annotated list of my favourite picture books, all of which have been 'road tested' with my children/grandchildren.

No-one doubts the value of reading poems and stories to children and a verse from Strickland Gillilan's poem 'The Reading Mother' neatly sums up its importance:

> You may have tangible wealth untold:
> Caskets of jewels and coffers of gold.
> Richer than I you can never be-
> I had a mother who read to me.

[quoted in Reid and Bentley, *Helping your child to read*, p2]

Story telling

Telling a story is, of course, very different from reading one. Being deprived of the prop of a book can be daunting. It's harder work, and needs preparation. You might also feel you couldn't possibly match the fluency of a written narrative. Well, maybe, but there are gains as well as losses: you don't have to keep looking at a book; all your attention can be devoted to your audience; and you can use your face, hands, and body in telling the tale.

Storytelling preparation

- It's probably best to start with a tale you know well, like 'Cinderella'. Get a clear outline of the main points and structure - those things without which the story falls apart. You have to mention the appearance of the Fairy Godmother, for example. And missing out the instruction about Cinderella returning before the clock strikes twelve leaves you with a real problem at the end of the Ball! You can say, 'I should have said earlier ..'. Alternatively, you can bluff it out, and say 'Now Cinderella had completely forgotten her Godmother's instruction to…'.

- Get a postcard, and reduce the main elements of the story (the absolutely essential points) to about 6 and write them down. Children won't mind if you occasionally use this as a crib; they're a very tolerant, understanding audience.

- A simple prop like a wand, or sword, or ring (any ring, wrapped in silver foil will do) is a great help. If you've got a number of characters, finger puppets are a good way of grabbing a child's attention.

- Don't forget the traditional stock phrases of fairy tales e.g. 'Once upon a time in a land far away', 'You shall go to the Ball, Cinderella', and 'They lived happily ever after'. The first one reminds us these stories never take place in a specific location, the last provides a comforting resolution.

- Involve your audience: ask questions like 'And what do you think happened next?' 'Have any of you seen an X, Y, or Z? This gives them a sense of shared ownership of the story (and ensures they're paying attention!). If you have forgotten what happens next, it also buys you time to rack your brains and/or improvise.

A story I particularly enjoy telling (perhaps because it always seems to have a contemporary social and political relevance) is 'The Emperor's New Clothes.' The naughtiness of the Emperor's nudity at the end of the tale appeals to children, and the teller is provided with wonderful opportunities for miming the stitching of (invisible) fine clothes and the Emperor's parading up and down 'wearing' them.

With growing confidence, you can start to make up your own stories, and whether you're reading or telling a story, children will be delighted if you incorporate their names within it. Your story may be a contemporary one woven around everyday events and the characters can include your children/grandchildren. If, on the other hand, you want your story to have a traditional fairy/folk tale flavour, you may find it helpful to draw on some of the stock characters and motifs of traditional fairy tales such as:

- A hero/heroine, and villain
- A journey or quest
- A prized goal which can only be achieved by overcoming obstacles
- A helper who gives the hero/heroine an object (which often has magical properties) to assist them in their quest

Some people, of course, are born storytellers. They have this natural ability to create stories, people them with interesting characters, and weave a spell over their listeners. I envy them. I don't possess this talent myself – neither, I'm guessing, do most of my readers – but we needn't let that stop us putting a bit of time and effort into developing and refining our storytelling skills.

Take the plunge! You may find you derive greater enjoyment from *telling* stories than reading them.

> It's possible to purchase books online that are tailored to a particular child (be warned – they are quite expensive!). They have attractive covers and are often printed on high-quality paper. In other words the book is personally commissioned: the child's name becomes the name of the principal character, and the story is woven around them. In theory it sounds irresistible; in practice I found them disappointing. The original 'bespoke' stories I looked at were anodyne, lacking inspiration, and invention. Once the novelty had worn off, I'm sure they'd be cast aside. Of course, the substitution of a child's name in a traditional story or folk tale is a different thing and something I've already recommended trying.

CHAPTER 4

Choosing Toys: Traditional v. Technological

'Sorry, Grandad, we're busy writing a new program.'

'It's your grandchild's birthday, or it's Christmas. Time for presents, and the ecstatic cries of pleasure of children unwrapping them. First choice for parents and grandparents is often a toy. You go to the toyshop (which looks very different from the last time you visited one 20 odd years ago) and are confronted by a bewildering range of seductive toys. How do you begin to make a choice? What kind of things should influence your decision?

The last 40 years have seen a transformation in kids' toys as traditional toys (often made of wood) were displaced in many homes by plastic, battery-powered toys with lots of 'bells and whistles'. Traditional toys have struggled in the face of fierce competition from these technological toys. The conflict is nicely dramatised in the Disney film, *Toy Story*. Woody, the cowboy puppet, has always been Andy's favourite. However, when a new birthday toy, Buzz Lightyear, a plastic astronaut, is introduced to the household, the spotlight falls on him. Woody desperately tries to regain both his owner's affection, and his role as the toys' leader. But it's hard going: Buzz has brightly coloured lights that flash on and off; a series of commands and responses that can be activated; and, best of all, his ability to 'fly to infinity and beyond.'

As one of a generation of boys who played the game of 'Cowboys and Indians' for hours on end, my sympathies are with Woody - at least for a time. One of the strengths of the film is it forces died-in-the wool toy traditionalists like me to acknowledge that kids today find inspiration for role-play games in the new heroes of popular culture: the astronaut, and the new super-heroes of films, television and comics. I find this change interesting because in ancient Greece – often regarded as the cradle of Western civilisation – superheroes were figures of enormous cultural significance. What goes around, come around!

Eventually, I succumbed to Buzz Lightyear's charm and warm-hearted nature and there's obviously a place for sophisticated battery-powered plastic toys in the child's toy cupboard. The plastic toy has an immediate 'Wow!' factor, but I can't resist the feeling that younger children are more engaged by wooden toys, and ultimately get greater satisfaction from them.

Let me try to sum up the respective pros and cons of these 2 types of toys:

Wooden toys

Pros:

- They are safe. It's difficult to see how children would be harmed by wooden toys (unless they're clobbered over the head with one - but then that would also apply to plastic toys).

- They are attractive to touch. One should never underestimate the tactile appeal of toys – and books.

- Well-made wooden toys are visually appealing.

- They play an important role in developing hand/eye co-ordination and children's manual dexterity. They also help children develop counting and grouping skills, as well as recognising the similarities between shapes in jigsaw puzzles (for example, where the child has to find where the matching car/boat/animal piece etc fits).

- They are very durable. It's almost impossible to break most wooden toys.

Cons:

I could only come up with one:

- They are expensive; certainly more expensive than all but the most sophisticated plastic, battery operated toys. This, of course, is because of the craftsmanship that's gone into their construction – they're labour-intensive.

Plastic battery-powered toys

The benefits of these toys tend to be more apparent with slightly older children – say from 24-30 months upwards.

Pros:

- The best plastic, battery operated toys offer considerable educational benefits because they permit high levels of interactivity. For example, children add different numbers, and are then told whether they have the right answer – or need to try again. Many also have jingles and songs operated by pressing a button, and children are invited to recite/sing along. Remember, though, if a toy doesn't retain the child's interest, its educational potential is likely to remain unfulfilled. The primary purpose of toys is to entertain; if they can help children learn at the same time, that's a real bonus.

- They're visually attractive – brightly coloured flashing lights make an immediate appeal.

- Many include a range of interesting sounds activated by turning a handle/pressing a button etc.

- A whole range of electronic toys/games are beginning to appear as apps that can be downloaded on a variety of platforms (mobile phones, Ipod, computers etc). Apps will be considered in the next section.

- They tend to be cheaper – though, I have noted sharp increases recently in the price of more sophisticated electronic toys.

Cons:

- They lack the tactile quality of wooden toys and are less likely to promote the development of motor co-ordination skills in young children than wooden toys that involve stacking, pushing, or hammering pegs in holes, and puzzles where the child has to identify and fit pieces in the appropriate shape.

In my experience, many plastic, electronic toys have an immediate appeal, but don't seem to engage the interest of younger children (roughly up to 3 years-old) for long. I've canvassed other parents and grandparents and they say the same thing. With older children, the sophisticated nature of these toys, and the possibilities they offer for narrative role-playing (many are spin-offs from TV series and films) assumes greater importance. This is where the versatile battery-operated toy comes into its own far more.

Visit any large toyshop or go online and it won't be long before you come across a display section with 'Educational' electronic toys. When I've looked closely at the educational benefits of these toys, I've always been sceptical about the more extreme claims made for them. My suspicions were confirmed by a *Which* magazine investigation (January 2012). The educational benefits that some companies claimed for their products, said *Which*, were vague and, at times, misleading. Naturally parents and grandparents are always on the lookout for toys that might enhance children's learning. However, a panel of *Which* education experts concluded that while toys like VTech Storio and Leapfrog LeapPad Explorer's 'nifty stylus' (both American toys) offered some educational benefits, it was almost inevitable that children interacting with these products would learn something. If parents wanted children to learn via an interactive computer-style toy, 'similar benefits could be gained more cheaply via child-friendly apps for an adult smartphone or tablet computer'. As the *Which* experts point out, children also learn from engaging in everyday activities like writing shopping lists and creating birthday cards, playing board games, drawing and reading.

It was interesting to note that in *The 100 Greatest Toys*, a Channel 4 programme hosted by Jonathan Ross in 2010, the toy voted the No 1 toy of all time was not an electronic toy or a TV spin-off toy, but Lego. Though Lego is made of plastic, it is a traditional constructional toy dating back to 1947, made by a Danish company who originally produced a wide range of wooden toys.

Most people would immediately think of their local *Early Learning Centre* or *Toys R Us* as the obvious places to look for wooden toys. However, it seems to me *Clementine Toys* has a wider selection, and I would definitely recommend you first try their very helpful website www.clementinetoys.com. Those living within striking distance of Southampton can visit their recently opened shop where they will not only be assured of an immensely pleasurable experience (reliving their youth!) but can also benefit from the owners' advice on selecting appropriate toys for different age groups.

Looking for plastic toys? You'll find a good selection in *Toys R Us*. And if your budget is limited, try the charity shops and car boot sales. You can pick up toys, games, and jigsaw puzzles in excellent condition very cheaply.

CHAPTER 5

The Perfect Babysitter? Apps, TV and DVDs

OK – what are apps? An app is an abbreviation for application – it's a piece of software that can run on your computer or mobile phone (Apple with its iPhone and iPad has been particularly quick to exploit this market). As a dyed-in-the-wool technophobe, I was sceptical about the benefits of the new range of smart phone apps. However, the development of educational apps designed to help children's language skills helped in overcoming my initial suspicion that they were just about marketing a new range of games.

But are we faced with a wider problem here. Is digital technology taking over our lives? Or, more precisely, the lives of our grandchildren? Teenagers walk around the streets with mobile phones clamped to their ears. When they're not phoning/texting friends on the bus, or train, there's a constant drip feed of music from their earphones. There seems to be a compulsive need for stimulation, and a dread of doing nothing, of just walking along or sitting down ... thinking about things. The Golden Rule is: thou must not be bored. However, I've often thought doing nothing - being bored - can be quite productive (my wife claims this is the rationalisation of a lazy man).

I bet when Archimedes jumped from his bath and shouted 'Eureka! I've suddenly realised a fundamental law about the displacement of water' it was precisely because he'd been doing nothing (apart, maybe, from contemplating his navel and the bathwater). My belief in the positive value of boredom (often the result of doing nothing) was confirmed by Sue Maushart's book, *The Winter of Our Disconnect*, (Maushart, 2011). Concerned about the social and educational well-being of her three teenage children (and herself), she decided to junk most forms of digital technology for a 6 month 'Experiment' (mobile phones and stereos were allowed). She identifies boredom as:

> a big issue for parents today. Not just listening to kids complain about boredom – but responding to those complaints ... and perhaps above all throwing technology at those complaints. Somewhere along the line, providing "stimulation" became a key aspect of our [parents] job

description. The belief that a stimulated child is an advantaged child is so widely shared we rarely bother to articulate it. So too, of course, is its corollary: that a bored child is an at risk child ... Even before The Experiment, I'd started to wonder whether we'd been confusing 'plugging in' with 'switching on'; whether boredom – far from being the enemy of all that is educational – might turn out to be our friend. [Maushart, 2011, p70]

Maushart's point about 'stimulation' struck a chord for me. Seeing my grandchildren surrounded by a mountain of toys, I wondered whether they were over-stimulated, especially when those toys were part of a programme of activities like painting, drawing, gym club, and ballet - not to mention DVDs, and TV. On the other hand, I don't want to become a 'grumpy old Luddite'. You can't 'un-invent' digital or any other kind of technology, nor would I wish to – especially when many apps are not only entertaining, but have a real educational value.

You may be thinking at this point: what has all this to do with younger children? If so, remember there are 7-year-olds with their own mobile phones, and an Ofcom report in 2012 revealed that over a third of pre-schoolers are going online using a PC, laptop or netbook. Many can find their way around these devices more skilfully than their grandparents!

In a move that surprised many, the British government recently acknowledged the centrality of computers in the lives of young children by advising parents and nursery schools that children should be introduced to computers from the age of 22 months.

Apps

Fleur Britten in a Sunday Times article pointed out that 60% of the iTunes App Store's top educational apps are designed for toddlers and preschoolers. Parents compete over whose child will be the first to display digital fluency: one boasts of her child's ability to unlock the iPhone; another counters with, 'Her first word was "Hello" while holding an imaginary phone to her ear.'

Apps and autism

What first convinced me of the potential value of apps was finding out about Lisa Domican, an Irish-based Australian mother with 2 autistic children, Liam and younger sister, Grace. Lisa's inspiring story deserves to be better known.

In a radio interview, Lisa explained that by the age of 2 neither of her children had begun speaking which is one of the first indicators of autism. Some autistic children learn to talk with a picture exchange system where the child associates a picture with something he or she wants e.g. a cookie. To obtain a cookie they hand over a picture of one, then they begin to learn the words that go with the pictures, and gradually progress to building sentences. Liam used the picture system for about 3 months with pictures attached by Velcro to cardboard pages in a book. After this, he was largely able to dispense with the picture book.

Unfortunately Lisa's daughter 'had no speech, no babble, hardly any eye contact' (Carers' Sanctuary Magazine). It became apparent Grace was more intensely autistic than her brother, and her school lacked the resources to give her all the help she needed. To work with Grace on a one-to-one basis, Lisa went on a course to teach her how to use picture books. Though Grace made rapid progress with the picture exchange system, she still didn't say a word. For several years, Lisa was printing pictures, laminating them, and attaching them to a book. During this period, her daughter's 'vocabulary' grew to the point where she had 400 pictures in a large A4 folder - and, of course, the book/folder was growing increasingly cumbersome.

The breakthrough came when Lisa saw an advert for an iPhone and realised its potential to help her daughter. The big, clumsy book could be abandoned because images could be put onto the iPhone, and swiftly accessed. But Lisa still lacked the technical expertise to translate her idea into an iPhone application. She found the name of a web developer and asked for his help. They arranged to meet in a shopping centre cafe, and when he said he'd get a lift from his dad, she wondered how old he was! 'He turns up', she said, 'he's 20. I had Gracie's book, I told him the story. I drew him a diagram and later that afternoon he emailed me a prototype of exactly what I'd been talking about.'

The new Grace App was simple, and worked in real time; it could be customised to the individual child using their picture and photo vocabulary. 'The phone is compact,' said Lisa, 'but can hold hundreds of images; and adding new images and sharing them with the parent/carer/tutor is simple and instant which encourages consistency in the language development of the child.'

This 'fairy tale' story has a happy ending. With generous sponsoring from Apple and O₂, the Grace app became a huge success. Enthusiastically promoted through a range of community education programmes, it won a United Nations World Summit Award for e-Learning and Education, and transformed the lives of many autistic children.

'App-iness, app-iness, the greatest tool that I possess'

Even if you set aside the educational benefits of apps, they still have a place in the repertoire of aids for parents and grandparents. You're in the doctor's waiting room, or an airport – or doing anything that absolutely requires your undivided attention? Send for App! Critics may bang on about the dangers of children becoming addicted to apps and TV, but what they forget is when you're exhausted, you'll resort to anything that buys you a little peace and quiet.

Whenever I'm tempted to say, 'Little Johnny or Mary shouldn't be allowed to do that,' I try to remember their mum or grandad may have had little sleep the night before (because they've been looking after little J or M) and are at the end of their tether. Sometimes survival is the name of the game. Warren Buckleitner, in a New York Times article on phone apps, points out that faced with a 3-year-old on the verge of full meltdown, you're naturally going to resort to the 'perfect, non-chemical tranquillizer.' And who can blame you? Incidentally, I think his advice applies to any child aged between 3 and 13!

The good news is many apps can be downloaded free. Of course, companies entice customers with free apps, hoping they'll be encouraged to purchase further titles. Unsurprisingly, there's usually a charge for the most popular apps but prices are modest so unless you get carried away on a buying spree, you're unlikely to spend a lot of money.

If you're dipping your toe in the app water for the first time, you may find a shortlist of recommended apps helpful. Of course, there are now hundreds of apps; this list only scratches the surface, and some will probably have disappeared by the time this book is published.

Recommended shortlist of Apps:

Wheels on the Bus
A favourite preschool song, this interactive musical book which 'encourages cognitive, linguistic, and motor development' (Sunday

Times review) also lets you record your own child singing. (ages 2-5)

Kid Art
As with most drawing apps, you choose a type of crayon, and off you go. Kid Art has over 20 different pre-drawn backgrounds and comes with a choice of cartoon animal and object stamps that you can add anywhere on your picture – children love those. You also get a choice of theme which alters the type of stamps and backgrounds available e.g. Under the Sea or At School.

My Very First App
Based on the beautiful illustrations of Eric Carle's famous *The Very Hungry Caterpillar*, this app has 3 levels of difficulty. Easy mode contains 2 stacked images, colours on top and images below. The child matches them by swiping back and forth until they line up, then an audible tone and a voice lets you know you've made a match. (ages 2-7)

Miss Spider's Tea Party
This charming animated story has an option where kids can read the story themselves or have it read aloud while touching the screen to watch superb 3D graphics. The app also offers easy jigsaw puzzles, and a fabulous colouring program. (ages 3 to 8)

Magic Piano
Kids are provided with different kinds of keyboards and can tap on the screen and hear notes. They can also select 'Songbook' and tap out a variety of well-known classical pieces such as Fur Elise and the Moonlight Sonata. You can set the difficulty level according to your piano expertise or your mood.

Drawing Pad
Cheaper and less messy than paints and felt-tips, this app has lots of art tools to choose from, including crayons, markers, paintbrushes and special markers that sprinkle shapes and stickers. Kids can save their 'paintings' or email them to friends. (age 4 and up) There are a number of apps with similar titles and rather than provide a long web address, I suggest you google: Drawing Pad – Android Apps for Google Play.

A cautionary note:

I'm uneasy about some much-loved children's books being made available as apps. There is, for example, an app of Lewis Carroll's *Alice in Wonderland*. One online review gives it his highest rating, and says, 'It has 52 illustrated pages containing 20 animated scenes where touching or tilting the iPad ... can make Alice grow or shrink.'

Surely the point about a great book is that it enables the child's, or adult's, imagination to go to work on an image or scene or emotion described by the author. Even with a picture book, the pictures may well be a springboard for creating further pictures in the 'reader's mind'. We speak of a writer painting a picture in words. The imagination can do far more than the most wonderful pictures on the screen and you aren't tied down to any particular visual representation. And the picture you create in your head may be very different from the one in mine.

I'm not alone: the best-selling children's writer, Julia Donaldson, dislikes the prospect of ebooks entirely taking over the children's book market and has vetoed an ebook version of *The Gruffalo*, her most famous book. I think Donaldson also recognises the danger of the book's narrative flow and rhythms being interrupted by digital distractions. Educationalists rightly emphasise the importance of sitting next to your child/children and sharing picture books with them. That sharing process crucially involves discussion of images ('what do you notice about the trees in Max's room in *Where the Wild Things Are*'?) because the meaning of a picture book so often resides in the **combination** of word and image. However, when the child is eager to find out what happens next, parents/ grandparent should avoid too much discussion. The rule is: respect the book, be sensitive to the narrative flow, and sparing with your interventions. As the wise old Dr Johnson once remarked, 'The mind becomes refrigerated by interruption'! You have to decide when to pause, question or discuss particular images, and when to move on swiftly. Such decisions are largely taken out of your hands with the app or ebook.

Perhaps because of the dominance of visual media in our culture generally, there's a tendency to think one must always create a visual equivalent for the printed word - that words on their own are somehow insufficient or inadequate. It's a tendency that should be resisted.

Some children's picture-books are works of art: a marvellous fusion of words and images. However, there are stories that work perfectly well without illustrations.

TV, Films and DVDs

By the time your grandchild is 2 years-old, you've probably found the urge to switch on Children's TV irresistible – especially if you're looking after children on a regular basis (i.e. one or more days a week).

Yes, I know you took a solemn vow not to succumb. Of course, you started with worthy intentions of being SUPERGRAN/GRAMPS. You were determined your grandchildren would be engaged in:

- Learning nursery rhymes
- Finger painting
- Planting cress in plastic pots on windowsills
- Making fairy cakes
- Constructing models out of washing-up bottles and corn flakes packets à la Blue Peter
- Learning to sing songs and play the piano
- Making up little plays to perform when Mum and Dad get home

However, you are now tired out. You've got their lunch. You've sorted their quarrels. You've changed their nappies, and cleared up the mess in the kitchen/lounge etc. Dammit, you just want to sit down and relax.

'Okay, kids ... let's switch on *Peppa Pig*! "Hooray!"'

So that's what you do. Welcome to the real world. Meanwhile a little devil is prodding your conscience with his pitchfork.

'You know they'll grow two heads? Be blind by their 3rd birthday? Have their reading age set back by 15 yrs? Make them into anti-social couch potatoes?'

And your right-on, liberal, PC friends are shocked when you let slip what you've done; they don't say anything but you know what they're thinking. Well, I've good news for you. None of the above will happen – leastways, not the devil's predictions. To live in harmony with children's television, you just need to remember two golden rules:

1. Moderation – as with most things in life, watching TV in moderation does you no harm (and that applies especially to good children's TV).

Watching 30 minutes is fine; a whole morning or afternoon isn't. Of course, the advent of dedicated satellite children's TV channels like CBeebies, Nick Junior, and Disney channel has fuelled fears children could end up watching from 7am to 7pm! No sensible person would advocate that.

2. Watch with your grandchildren/children. This is very important. Talk to them about what is happening – certainly the first time round. Kids love watching programmes, or stories, over and over again so by the time you get to the 3rd screening of the same *Peppa Pig* episode that interaction with you may be less important. And let them see you're enjoying the programme as much as they are - not difficult in the case of Peppa Pig!

Critics of television often make the mistake of assuming that watching TV is a passive activity. But even if kids aren't watching with an adult, they are still anticipating what's going to happen next; empathising with characters; reflecting on what has happened; and (to a minor extent maybe) questioning and forming judgements e.g. was that a bad action? Do I sympathise with this character? All the kinds of responses we would expect from a child listening to, or reading, a story.

Frankly, I've never understood the knee-jerk condemnation of children's TV. It tends to go hand in hand with a suspicion of TV in general, a conviction that it represents the bastardisation of our culture by American media institutions. Television is blamed for everything: the decline in literacy, poor educational performance, and rising levels of violence in society. Such criticisms are invariably extended to other forms of digital media.

Whilst I *am* concerned – like Maushart - about the way digital media is taking over the lives of teenagers, I don't feel this criticism should be applied indiscriminately to all TV. There are bad children's programmes, and there are also a lot of excellent ones. Years ago, I remember a colleague telling me he wouldn't allow his teenage kids to watch the long-running school series *Grange Hill* because it would encourage them to use bad language (swearing, he meant). However, having watched *Grange Hill* regularly over a period of nine or ten years, and taught it on a media studies course, I knew it contained no swearing. Perhaps his assumption had more to do with the kids' use of slang and colloquial language.

The BBC and 50 years of classic children's TV

The BBC can be justly proud of its children's TV output. For over 50 years, it has produced outstanding programmes – particularly programmes for pre-school children. A roll call of classic programmes for the very young would include: *Andy Pandy*, Sooty, *The Fowerpot Men* (Bill and Ben), *The Woodentops, Camberwick Green, The Clangers, Bagpuss, Trumpton, Ivor the Engine, Fireman Sam, Vision on*, and *Take Hart* [apologies if I've missed out any of your favourites].

The last two – *Vision on* and *Take Hart* – were important landmarks because they were designed to appeal to both hearing and deaf children. *Vision on* presented by Pat Keysell and Tony Hart was a very visual programme with little or no speech. The programme which mixed art, animation, clowning and dangerous stunts, launched the careers of David Sproxton who later created Aardman Animations (of Wallace and Gromit fame) and Sylvestor McCoy who became the seventh Dr Who. *Vision On* lasted for over 10 years, and was succeeded by *Take Hart* which showcased Tony Hart's artistic skills in encouraging kids to be creative with a wide range of materials.

More recently, there has been the phenomenally successful *Teletubbies*, *In the Night Garden*, and *Peppa Pig*. The *Teletubbies* generated huge controversy both here and in the US. The main thrust of this in Britain was that the Tubbies' nonsense language impaired young children's language development, and was part of a tendency towards dumbing-down.

Obviously critics had forgotten the nonsense language of Bill and Ben (and Weed) in the *Flowerpot Men*, as well as those delightful creatures, the *Clangers*. Most educationalists now acknowledge, the *Teletubbies* had a beneficial effect on children's language development. Anne Wood, the programme's creator, was an experienced teacher and child psychologist. The philosophy of the show, she argued, was defiantly child-centred, and young children learnt not through instruction but play. In fact this playful attitude is what characterises all the programmes in the list above, and makes them so enchanting for both children and adults. In contrast to what some critics argued, children were able to make sense of what Laa-Laa, Tinky Winky, Dipsy, and Po were saying from the inflections and rhythm of their utterances, as well as the dramatic context.

I have to thank my grandchildren for introducing me to *Peppa Pig* and *In the Night Garden*. *Peppa Pig* deals with everyday situations children can identify with like a river trip, attending ballet class, going for a walk on a wet day and splashing in puddles). Children and grown-ups respond to humour that's sometimes simple, and sometimes, surprisingly sophisticated. In one episode Daddy Pig makes a hash of putting up a picture, and tries desperately to conceal the damage before Mummy Pig returns. I know one adult who's faced that particular crisis.

In the Night Garden is another hugely successful programme from Anne Wood. Described by its makers as 'a magical picture book place that exists between eating and sleeping', each episode has a final section where the day's activities are recounted and each character is tucked up in bed. As one critic comments, the show is structured as 'the perfect winding down activity before you send the little ones to sleep.'

For many children *In the Night Garden* clearly acts as a comfort blanket, a ritualistic prelude to bedtime. As for me – well, I'm captivated by the psychedelic colours, and the surreal, magical atmosphere.

The popularity of animated programmes in children's TV scheduling has been matched in recent years by Justin Fletcher – better known as Mr Tumble. Justin had appeared in a variety of children's programmes, and 'voiced' characters like Shaun in *Shaun the Sheep*, and Harold in *Thomas, the Tank Engine*.

In the period 2009-12, he created 3 series – *Gigglebiz, Something Special*, and *Justin's House* – each of which became an instant hit. *Gigglebiz*, a series that launched characters like Anna Condor, the reptile house warden, and Gail Force, the TV weather presenter, was a mixture of comedy sketches and jokes told by children.

It was *Something Special*, however, featuring Mr Tumble, that established his reputation as the clown prince of British children's television. Mr Tumble's circus clown's clothes and make-up (freckles, red nose) reflect Fletcher's love of slapstick and clowning. Unsurprisingly, his heroes are the slapstick legends of early cinema – Buster Keaton, Charlie Chaplin, and Laurel and Hardy.

In some ways *Something Special* and *Justin's House* can be seen as successors to *Vision On* and *Take Hart*. Like these programmes, Justin is clearly committed to reaching out to children with speech and learning difficulties. In *Something Special* he switches between being Mr Tumble and 'Justin'. Both he and the child participants (all of whom have some kind of disability) use Makaton sign language to accompany speech. Makaton signs (derived from the deaf community) are complemented by actions, symbols, and gestures. Justin is delighted with the feedback he's received about children who've spoken for the first time after watching the programme.

The first children's presenter to win a BAFTA, Justin was awarded an MBE in 2008 for his services to children's TV and the charity sector. According to a Daily Mail article, the Queen is a fan (she watches his programmes with her young grandchildren) and as she handed Fletcher his MBE, said, 'Well done and keep up the good work.'

I'd have no hesitation recommending any of these programmes – new or old – to parents and grandparents. Nearly all can be found on CBeebies, or other dedicated children's channels; alternatively, many are available as DVDs.

Something that's amazed me has been the way my two granddaughters have fallen under the spell of television and (DVD) films. It's almost impossible to break, as if fairy dust has been sprinkled over them. You can dance up and down, wave your arms, sing, pull funny faces - all to no avail. They remain oblivious to your presence, locked into the world created by film-makers, their gaze riveted on the screen.

It's a salutary reminder of the power of audio-visual storytelling. Is it something to worry about? I don't know!

Film and DVD

While children still occasionally see films at a cinema, they'll usually watch them on television. As a grandparent, you'll probably inherit a stack of DVDs, and be faced with insistent demands to 'Play this one!' If there are 2 or more siblings, penny to a pound they won't agree on the same DVD.

You may have no direct input, but you can still buy DVDs for your grandchildren or recommend particular films to their parents. The task then is to persuade the kids to watch them. If your instincts are sound and you like the film, that shouldn't be a problem.

When you think of fairy tales and classic children's films, you think of

Disney. The lustrous colours and inventive animation of early classics like *Snow White and the 7 Dwarfs*, *Sleeping Beauty*, and *Bambi* have rarely been matched by later films - though I do have a soft spot for *The Jungle Book*, *Robin Hood*, and *101 Dalmations*. Whatever you think about Walt Disney, he not only knew about animation, he knew how to tell a story.

Walt died in 1966 and, while the success of Disney studios' films continued unabated, there was mounting criticism of their portrayal of women (passive damsels in distress waiting for a prince to come and rescue them) and of non-white characters. In the last 2 decades, however, Disney Studios has responded to these accusations by trying to incorporate more positive portrayals of young women, and non-white races in their films. These efforts met with some success: *Beauty and the Beast* has a feisty heroine, and a male chauvinist 'villain' – it's just a shame the charismatic Beast eventually turns into a conventionally handsome but anodyne prince. Thankfully, in *Shrek*, Pixar's witty subversion of fairy tale conventions, there's no such transformation of the ugly yet appealing hero. Disney's *Pocahontas*, tries to be PC but the racist 'baddie' is British which conveniently lets America (and its exploitation of native American Indians) off the hook.

These days almost every children's film is a CGI (computer generated imagery) animated film. The success of the first CGI film, *Toy Story*, spawned a host of CGI animation films voiced by well-known actors, the best of which are probably *Shrek, Finding Nemo, Madagascar, Ice Age*, and *Up*.

A notable exception to the domination of CGI movies is *Mulan*, which employs the traditional mode of animation. Based on a Chinese folk tale, it tells the story of a heroine who refuses to accept the submissive role assigned to her by her father, and her culture. She falls in love with a prince whom she rescues from death, and later saves her father from disgrace and humiliation. Visually the film is impressive: one spectacular sequence depicts thousands of Huns sweeping down a snowy mountain. Disney Studios were careful to ensure this film ticked all the right PC boxes, and even though there seems to be something formulaic about its positive messages, my grandchildren love it.

These are, of course, the judgements of an adult; I'm sure children will be uncritical of these films, and probably enjoy all of them. Who knows, though, what messages they are unconsciously assimilating?

CHAPTER 6

'Are we nearly there yet?'

'Are we nearly there yet?'

We're all familiar with this refrain on car journeys. So how do you respond to it? Well, you can buy a set of Usborne cards with ideas for keeping kids entertained (they contain a few useful suggestions) and there are plenty of websites devoted to the problem but they often seem designed with older children in mind, and many of the activities suggested are more appropriate for ships or trains where you'll usually have more space, and can sit at a table.

The question 'Are we nearly there yet' (repeated at 5 minute intervals over a period of hours) is far more likely to grate in a car. Cars are – like aeroplanes which I'll come to later – a special case. A ship's a novelty. It has all kinds of areas for you to explore: you can move from deck to deck or sit at a table in a café area with a drink. Trains can be quite relaxing too – there are often tables where kids can draw or do puzzles (and, if you're lucky, a buffet car).

Neither trains nor ships are plagued by traffic jams; you don't get that claustrophobic feeling with kids and adults in close proximity in a car. And they don't have a driver desperately trying to concentrate on contra-flows and cones amidst the ear-piercing din of tired, fractious children.

As for aeroplanes ... well, don't get me started. You have the awful car journey that precedes the hell of airports; then the interminable delays, the heat, and the endless queues. And when you've boarded the plane, you've got to put up with the same cramped conditions as a car. Sorry - all you can do on a plane is rely on the tablet computer, the app, the iPod, or the good old-fashioned book/magazine.

Of course, parents are more likely to be confronted by these problems than grandparents. On the other hand, we often have the time and the resources to take grandchildren out for day trips and even on holiday. And parents have always been happy to invite us to join them on family holidays. There are few things more pleasurable than helping your grandchildren build sand castles or watching their first efforts to swim in the sea . And we make ideal babysitters when parents want to go out for a meal or sample the night-life!

Keep it simple

With young children on a car journey my advice would be: keep it simple. Usually the driver will be invited (press-ganged?) to join in, so you want something that doesn't require too much thought or concentration. Don't dismiss 'I Spy' – it might bore you, but it's easy and young children enjoy it.

Other cars can be used in various ways. Count the number of red cars you pass; the winner is the first to reach 10 (repeat with other colours). Move on to particular makes of cars: Ford, Nissan, Toyota etc, and bicycles and prams in towns. Ring the changes with lorries, vans, car transporters, and – in rural areas – tractors!

Here are some other ideas:

20 Questions
One person thinks of an animal or object and the other players can ask a total of 20 questions to try and identify it.

What's my line
Older readers (sorry – I mean more mature readers) will remember this TV panel game from the 50s. One person thinks of a job (e.g. teacher, postman/woman, nurse, doctor, farmer etc) and the others can ask a total of 10 questions to try and identify it. With younger children, it may be better for an adult to choose the occupation, and the children ask the questions. Once they get the hang of it, kids can choose the job.

Car number plate abbreviations
[Perhaps more suitable for children aged 5-7 and upwards!]

Try to make a 3 word phrase from the number plate letters you see on passing vehicles. For example, my VLB plate could be 'very lovely bananas' or 'vicious little bandits'. Players choose their personal favourite from the responses – but there are no winners. You could be flexible with 'X' and allow 'eXciting', 'eXtreme', 'eXtraordinary' etc.

'Left field' ideas
It's surprising how the most unlikely things will work. I remember long car journeys to Woolacombe many years ago for the annual family holiday. My two kids were getting bored, as Dad set off on another diversion to try to escape traffic jams. The air became shrill with 'Are we nearly there yet?' Suddenly we passed a breakdown lorry towing a car. Dad – desperate – asked them, 'What happens when a breakdown lorry breaks down?' Pause. 'You get a breakdown lorry to tow the breakdown lorry to tow the car home'. 'But what happens if that breakdown lorry breaks down?' Continue for as long as it has legs, which in this case was an amazingly long time! The mere mention of a breakdown lorry 35 years later is enough to start my family reminiscing.

On another occasion (en route to Woolacombe again), a diversion had taken us deep into the heart of farming country. We were all hungry; Dad had been searching for a pub that gave him the right 'vibes' about its food, and those vibes were still to be activated. Then we passed a farm worker in traditional farming attire. 'Ooh, look,' I said. 'A country bumpkin!' Again, I had no idea this would provoke hilarious laughter, but it kept my little smashers giggling and repeating this phrase (relishing, of course, its rude associations) for some time afterwards.

So, in desperate situations, the most unlikely things can prove a source of entertainment for kids. And, if everything else fails, there's always either a CD of kids' songs (where everyone can join in) and stories, or the more expensive solution: computer/iPad games.

CHAPTER 7

'Food, glorious food!'

'...and let your grandchildren help in the preparation of food.' (p.64)

Hardly a day goes by without some new report about rising levels of obesity in children and adults. In 2011, the Telegraph reported that researchers at Swansea University had found 8% of girls and 5% of boys were classified as obese before their 5th birthday! Four years earlier, the Medical Research Council (a government funded body) said if current trends persisted, one in 5 children would be overweight. The main causes of obesity were thought to be (not unexpectedly) poor diet and lack of exercise.

What can parents and grandparents do to address this problem? Clearly, the responsibility of grandparents for feeding grandchildren varies considerably. Obviously when both parents are working, it's more likely you may be called upon to provide food.

What do you give your grandchildren to ensure they have a healthy balanced diet? Well, to begin with, you can't go wrong with fruit and vegetables – I don't think it always needs to be 5 pieces per day (the government has rowed back a little on that prescription) but it's a good target to aim for. You can make large batches of healthy soup, freeze use-able quantities, and whip them out (Oh God, I'm lapsing into Jamie-speak) as required. There's no shortage of recipe books with sections on soup and there's an endless supply online.

If you're buying convenience meals from supermarkets always check amounts of fat (especially saturated fat), sugar, and salt. Nearly all supermarkets now use colour-coded labels: choose either orange (medium levels) or green (low); never buy red labelled products.

Remember: most parents are time-poor; you're probably time-rich. So if you're responsible for feeding your grandchildren, you don't have to rely on take-aways and convenience meals. You can make batches of cottage pie or spaghetti Bolognese for the freezer; these can be heated up later in the microwave, leaving you free to keep tabs on the kids. Fish is quick and easy to prepare and, as long as you don't have it too often, it's good for you. Of course, fish doesn't always have to mean fish fingers. My wife and I have returned to an old supper favourite which our grandchildren love: smoked haddock – just pop a poached or fried egg on top, serve with frozen peas. You've got a healthy dish fit for a queen and it's ready in 10 minutes.

Kids (and adults) often turn their noses up at salads but there are lots of ways to pep up salads and make them really attractive. You can cheat and buy those ready-washed bags of leaves, make up an interesting (low fat) dressing, and add ham, cooked chicken, or smoked mackerel (oily fish are the healthiest). And don't forget that marvellous standby: hard-boiled eggs! There always seem to be some eggs in the house so you rarely have to make a trip to the shops.

Reluctant eaters

I've no worries about my grandchildren being over-weight. Quite the reverse. It's been more about getting them to eat perfectly healthy food. Childcare experts maintain that as long as children are active, are not losing weight, and look healthy, we don't need to worry; they will eat when they are hungry. I'm sure they are right, but it's natural to be concerned – especially when one child wolfs down everything put in front of her, and another studiously ignores his food.

At this point, Grandad resorts to a few old tricks:

'You know if you eat your peas it'll make your eyes sparkle? Watch.' [Grandad manically flutters his eyelashes and blinks]

Or

'I bet you can't eat one more spoonful of that lovely X. I bet he can't, Grandma. Wow! That's amazing. But you won't be able to eat another one/two/three, will you? [don't push too hard, especially if the child's eaten a reasonable portion]

Another ploy when kids turn their noses up without trying X is to make it very clear you want this DELICIOUS dish.

'That looks fantastic. Mmmm.... Can I eat yours?' Invariably the reply is, 'No, it's mine!' Nothing increases the desirability of something faster than someone else wanting it. I don't tell my grandchildren but usually I can't wait to get my hands on their food! It's a win-win situation: if I succeed and they eat their food, I'm happy; and if I get lucky and they leave it, I'm happy.

If all else fails, try using the kind of theatrical deception techniques I discussed in Chapter 2. The other day at lunchtime my grandson said he didn't want his yoghurt. 'Why?' I asked him. Yoghurt is normally the prize with which we entice him to eat the 'main course'.

My grandson is one of those kids who is constantly hungry ('I want a biscuit/banana/chocolate bar' etc) but - when it comes to lunchtime – his appetite mysteriously disappears. I expect you know the type.

My wife placed the strawberry yoghurt in front of him. 'Come on, this is your favourite'. 'Don't like it', he replied. 'I want a chocolate yoghurt'.

Now I don't think they make a chocolate yoghurt – a mousse certainly, but not a yoghurt. I wracked my brains and suddenly had an idea.

'I think there is a chocolate yoghurt in the fridge,' I said to my wife, winking furiously. She looked at me blankly. 'No, there's not'.

'Don't you remember, darling – we put one in there yesterday'.

My wife continued to ignore my frantic gestures. I went over, replaced the Peppa Pig strawberry yoghurt, and made a great show of ferreting in the fridge (one of those huge American jobs).

'Ah, here we are,' I said to my grandson. 'There's a strawberry one with lots of chocolate bits in it. If you don't want it, I'll have it!'

Needless to say, the strawberry yoghurt (with choccy bits) was gratefully accepted – and rapidly consumed.

In my mind, I was triumphantly punching the air, shouting 'YEAHH!' and shamefully relishing my ability to outwit a 3 year-old. My wife – as if reading my thoughts – looked on disapprovingly. Unabashed, I compared my con-man efforts favourably with those of Robert Redford and Paul Newman in *The Sting* movie and the hustlers in the TV series *Hustle*.

I moved in for the kill. 'Did you like that yoghurt?' I asked.

'Yes'.

'What flavour was it?'

'You know what flavour it was Grandad – strawberry with chocolate bits'.

Game, set, and match to Grandad.

A sense of houmous?

When my wife and I were bringing up our children (in the late 1960s and early 70s) it would never have occurred to us to give them houmous or olives, because a) we'd never heard of houmous, and b) olives were regarded with some suspicion as those foreign hors d'oeuvres served at posh parties. But houmous and olives are exactly what our daughter gave her children from a fairly early age and our granddaughter, in particular, loved them!

My daughter's philosophy is clear: what she likes, her daughter will probably like. We may be too ready to assume young children won't like highly flavoured or unusual food. Too conservative an attitude can lead to children becoming 'picky'. As long as highly flavoured food is healthy, I don't think anything should be regarded as 'off-limits'. Contemporary Britain is a multi-cultural society and our cuisine is a melting pot of culinary influences from all over the world. Walk down a typical high street and you'll see Italian, Indian, Chinese, and Spanish restaurants (as well as fusion this and fusion that). When a small child sees Mum and Dad eating pizza, or chicken tikka massala, they'll naturally want to try it.

A time to eat (together)

Children like routines; they like to know where they stand. Meal times should follow a fairly regular pattern with the day punctuated by breakfast, a mid-morning snack, lunch, mid-afternoon something-or-other, and tea – and finally bath-time and a story. With very young children, this daily routine usually includes a sleep during the morning and/or after lunch. Though there will inevitably be exceptions to this pattern, generally it needs to be adhered to. Too many disruptions to the routine are likely to lead to disruptive behaviour.

These are lessons one learns as a parent. They are handed down from one generation to another. So looking after grandchildren should simply be a matter of maintaining a routine established by parents. If it's not, then I'd suggest a tactful discussion with parents. If they're firmly opposed to this kind of routine, you've got a problem - but I think it's unlikely they will be. It's also important that – as far as possible – you eat together. The benefits of eating together are now widely accepted. Susan Maushart refers to research which shows a consistent correlation between family meals and positive outcomes for children:

> And not just slightly positive outcomes. Ridiculously positive ones. Kids who eat family meals five to seven times a week get better grades, have a sunnier outlook on life, have significantly fewer problems with drugs, alcohol, or nicotine, and seem almost magically protected from developing eating disorders. (*The Winter of our Disconnect*, p214)

So when your grandchildren want to eat in front of the TV, you tell them firmly, 'No'. There were times, Maushart admits, when she'd have been happy to read a newspaper or magazine, but she noted a radical improvement in communication, trust and understanding between members of the family when they all eat together. Working couples will often struggle to keep to family meals throughout the week, but that still leaves the weekend.

I must admit that until a couple of years ago, my wife and I frequently opted for an evening meal in front of the 'telly'. Then I decided to make a conscious effort to sit on an upright chair at a table. Almost immediately I started to enjoy my food more and it certainly aided digestion. TV suppers are now a rarity.

So children benefit from routines, and meals sitting with the family become part of that ritual of mealtimes that's such an integral part of French and Italian culture. The distractions of TV or the computer are removed and – most important of all – parents/grandparents get a chance to **interact and talk** to their children/grandchildren. Part of the ritual also involves observing a few conventions: you don't get down from the table until you've finished your meal; you don't speak with your mouth full; you don't try to put too much food in your mouth; and you are polite to others.

'Can we make cupcakes, Grandad?'

Kids enjoy making things in the kitchen - sometimes, of course, a chaotic mess! Encourage them; make cooking, and rustling up enticing dishes a family fun experience. The trouble is, as soon as you mention cooking and kids to parents or grandparents, they tend to think of chocolate rice crispies and cup cakes. In fact, most people's concept of child-friendly recipes seems to involve food high in fat or sugar.

It has a lot to do with safety considerations. Anything involving knives and chopping, or cooking on hobs, is automatically excluded. But you can still undertake these tasks and your grandchildren can help in the preparation of food. Take chicken nuggets, for example: after you've cut up free range chicken breasts into nuggets or fingers (you can substitute fish for chicken) the kids can dip them in beaten egg, and then roll them in seasoned breadcrumbs before you pop them under the grill for 10 to 15 minutes or a mark 5 (190° C) oven for 15-20 minutes. If you've more than one helper, they can form a conveyor belt! The result is a healthy meal everyone will enjoy – a world apart from the commercially produced infamous 'Turkey Twizzlers' exposed by Jamie Oliver.

If you want to eliminate knives entirely from the preparation of chicken nuggets, you can buy free range chicken mini-fillets already cut up into bite-sized portions. The only trouble is you pay more for the convenience. And while the chicken doesn't have to be free range, I do agree with Jamie Oliver: chickens reared in cramped factory farming conditions should be avoided.

What needs to be stressed is that cooking is FUN. Whether you're talking about children or adults, the best, most effective learning takes place when you're having fun and actively engaged in something. Kids can learn about: healthy, nutritional eating - why some foods are good for you, and others harmful; basic cookery skills that even under 5s can master; and where different foods come from.

All these issues (as well as others like 'Playing with pots and pans' and 'Pasta jewellery') are covered in the 'Cooking with Kids' section on Netmums' marvellous website: www.netmums.co.uk – it's a site I can unreservedly recommend. Another website worth checking out is the BBC's cbeebies site. You'll find scores of child-friendly recipes, (many of which have previously appeared on the *I can Cook* TV programme) plus information about different foods, and food-related games.

There must be over 50 recipe books for children. I've only carried out a small, completely unscientific survey, but 3 I've found particularly useful are:

The Big Book of Recipes for Babies, Toddlers & Children: 365 Quick, Easy and healthy Dishes by Bridget Wardley and Judy More, pub. Duncan Baird (like the other 2 books, this has many recipes that adults as well as children would enjoy, and includes such exotic dishes as minted beef samosas and marinated lamb kebabs)

New Complete Baby and Toddler Meal Planner by Annabel Karmel, pub. Ebury Press

The Top 100 Recipes for Brainy Kids by Christine Bailey, pub. Duncan Baird (there's a come-on title for you!)

These are recipe books for adults to cook for children but – following the advice on Netmums website - there's no reason why kids shouldn't be involved in the preparation of food.

There's only one way to end this chapter: 'Enjoy!'

CHAPTER 8

'Come on-a my house': Looking after Grandchildren in your Home

You may be looking after grandchildren in your home rather than theirs. Perhaps it's more convenient - or you just prefer it that way. You might have a garden to play in, whereas their own home doesn't; or there's more space for children to spread themselves. Also, you know where things are in your kitchen, and you have your own comfy chairs!

Your grandchildren are probably very happy with this arrangement: going to grandad's house is a novelty, an adventure. There are new places to explore – and, believe me, they will want to explore. On the other hand, there could be drawbacks. Your kitchen, for example; it's well-equipped, but do you have non-spill cups (they're essential), child-friendly cutlery, and booster seats/high chairs for very young children? However confident you are that it will be easy-peasy, a breeze, you need to prepare for their visit - whether it's a one-off or something that'll happen on a regular basis.

Preparing for a visit

While I don't want to encourage a siege mentality, you do need to batten down the hatches, and prepare for the invasion with almost military precision! The first thing you have to ensure is that you've child-proofed your home and created a safe environment:

- The most dangerous area of the house is probably the kitchen. Obviously, knives/knife blocks should be inaccessible. Don't allow chairs anywhere near worktops. Keep things like bleach, household cleaners completely hidden and – if possible - get hold of childproof cupboard locks. There are different types, they're inexpensive, and very easy to fit. Unfortunately, the ones on my daughter's cupboard doors are as much a deterrent to me as my grandchildren!
Place saucepans on the back burners of your cooker and make sure electric kettles are almost impossible for little hands to reach. Use plastic cups (for them) and be vigilant whenever there's glass about. Have regular sessions where you warn children of these dangers and strictly forbid any charging around in the kitchen: kitchen floors are

invariably hard and unforgiving.

- Make sure you've done everything possible to protect kids from hard, sharp edges. For example, we have a fireplace in our living room that we thought might be a potential hazard. If a young child fell on the hard stone surface it could be very painful or even cause serious injury. The problem was largely overcome by placing a round-edged, heavy coffee table against it. It was still possible for accidents to occur but this tended to keep grandchildren at a safe distance, and if you become too obsessive about safety, you'll make your and your grandchild's life a misery.

- For children under 3 you must have stair gates at the top and bottom of stairs. Unless there are particular reasons why older children still need this protection, the gates should be removed – though clearly this is something that needs discussing with the child's parents. It's important that children – like adults - become aware of, and assess, potential risks and dangers; it's part of growing up. However, if children are also spending the night in your house, there's a powerful argument for reinstating the gate at the top of the stairs. Waking up at night in a strange house is a disorientating experience and there is always the danger of sleepwalking (something I've experienced with my own grandchildren): **better to be safe than sorry!**

- Make sure you have some of their favourite books available, toys, games and jigsaw puzzles, and some paints, crayons, and paper (you can't go wrong with painting and colouring). It's probably best to confine colouring activities to the kitchen and, of course, only use washable paints and felt-tipped pens. You can – like David Hockney – 'paint' with computer programmes (see recommended Apps, chapter 4) but I still prefer the tactile pleasure of real paint. Just make sure plastic aprons are worn! And while your grandchildren's parents will probably have all the above items, and plenty of books and toys, it's still nice to build up your own library of children's books (see chapter 3) and a 'treasure trove' of toys, puzzles, and craft materials that are always ready to hand.

- Move treasured ornaments well out of arms' reach – we tend to put ours on a high bookshelf. Similarly, objects like table lamps that are easily knocked over, should be put somewhere safe.

- Try to build in treats – even if it's only a trip to the park, a walk in the woods, or a bus journey. My wife and I are fortunate. We live close to a lovely park where we take our three-year-old grandson. He likes to feed the ducks, play on the climbing frame, the swings and the roundabouts – and then go to the local coffee house in the nearby shopping precinct. He hasn't graduated to cappuccinos yet, but he clearly enjoys the bustling atmosphere of the coffee house (and the people who make a fuss of him). So he's happy, we're happy – it's a win-win situation.

- If they are staying overnight, don't forget their toothbrushes, flannels, pyjamas, and – whether or not it's a sleep-over – a potty for a baby, and a toilet training seat for a toddler.

I feel it's important you and your grandchildren are able to relax and enjoy their visit. So don't be too house-proud, or worried about what havoc they might wreak in your prized garden. Accept the fact that there will be accidents (whilst still attempting to anticipate and forestall them). If, in their excitement, they spill drinks or tread dirt into your carpets, don't get agitated or overreact. You want them to look back on their visit with warmth and enthusiasm, not remember grandad getting apoplectic about them trampling over his flower beds: people come before possessions.

Above all, regard your grandchildren's visit as an opportunity to involve them in your life. You suddenly find you've no little treat for a mid-morning break? Fine: ask them to help you make some cakes.

And if there are jobs around the garden that really need doing – like planting out those seedlings? Well let them help you. After that, you can take them round the garden, pointing out the popular names of plants – this one, for example, people call 'bunny rabbit' (or 'snapdragon'). *They're called this because when you squeeze the sides of the flower, the front opens to form a mouth... now these are 'Love-in-a-mist' (or Nigella).* Other flowers with interesting names that reflect their appearance or where they grow, are 'Baby's breath' (Gypsophelia), Red-Hot Poker' (Kniphotia), the 'Bell flower' (Campanula) and 'Lily of the Valley' (Convalleria).

Of course, there is a wealth of folklore attached to plants, some of it fanciful (often associated with magic and fairies), some more grounded in reality, focusing on the plant's reputed medicinal properties. You probably played that game as a child with dandelion globes where you blew the seeds off the globe and chanted 'She/he loves me, she loves me not'. The last seed to be blown away determined whether or not you were loved. Alternatively, the number of times it took to blow all the seeds off the dandelion globe was the hour number. The dandelion is also known as a rustic oracle because – it's claimed – its flowers always open about 5 in the morning, and close at 8 the evening.

Sometimes the medical and supernatural co-exist in a single plant. In Wales, for example, foxgloves (digitalis) – used in drug preparations for the treatment of heart problems - are believed to be a favourite lurking place for fairies. The plant is supposed to make a 'snapping sound when children, holding one end of the digitalis bell, suddenly strike the other end on the hand to hear the clap of thunder' (Wikipedia).

The tradition of associating plants with faery lore and folk medicines stretches back to Shakespeare *(A Midsummer Night's Dream, Hamlet, The Winter's Tale)* and beyond. You can help your grandchildren connect with the past, and also interest them in becoming young gardeners in the present. And if you don't have a garden, they can always grow cress in egg boxes on a window sill and plants in window boxes.

Children love looking at photos: I expect you've got photos of your children when they were young, and of your grandchildren as babies. Discuss those with them – they are bound to be fascinated and have lots of questions. Remember, that – in a very real sense - you are the custodian of family history and it's a history your grandchildren will enjoy sharing with you.

CHAPTER 9

'Are you our *real* Grandparents?'

Divorce and Grandparents

The increase in divorce rates over the last 2 or 3 decades has dramatically altered the grand-parenting landscape. With more people getting divorced, children are often faced with the bewildering situation of having not just one or two sets of grandparents, but multiple sets. Most people are familiar with the problems at Christmas of dividing their time between their own parents and their in-laws. Do I spend Christmas Day with my parents and Boxing Day with my wife's, or vice-versa?

If it's difficult for parents as they struggle with expanding family networks, what's it like for grandparents – and their relationships with their grandchildren – when parents get divorced? If each partner remarries, the likelihood of grandparents being denied access to grandchildren – or finding it very difficult – increases. And grandparents, unlike parents, have no legal right to access. The fact that two popular soap operas – BBC1's *Doctors* and BBC Radio 4's *The Archers* – have recently focused on the plight of grandparents in this situation, indicates it's a growing problem.

However many sets of grandparents there are, the temptation for you to somehow engineer more time with your grandchildren than other grandparents can be very strong. Though understandable, it's a temptation you should resist because it puts an unfair strain both on the child/children, and the parents. The situation requires tact, restraint and sensitivity, and the emotional and practical needs of the child must remain paramount. Ask yourself the question: 'Am I automatically assuming my right to see my grandchildren takes precedence over other grandparents?' How would you feel if the situation were reversed? Try to see things from their point of view, not just yours.

Kinship carers

For some grandparents the question 'Are you our *real* grandparents?' may be pertinent in a very different way. Far from being denied access to their grandchildren, they can find themselves in the role of primary carer – taking over as parent, assuming all the responsibilities of a parent. There could be various reasons for this, such as the death of one or both parents, drug dependency, or mental health problems. Rather than see a child taken into care, a grandparent (or in some cases other relative/close friend) may decide to step in and act as a primary carer. Whether you regard this as a rewarding challenge, a burdensome obligation, or somewhere in-between, will probably depend on a number of factors: your age, the age of the children, your income, your closeness to your grandchildren etc.

Even if the prospect of looking after grandchildren – possibly small grandchildren – full time, fills you with delight, you are probably going to find it an exhausting experience, especially if you are elderly. In a recent *Women's Hour* programme devoted to this problem, a grandmother who'd left a well-paid job to look after her grandchild, talked about the pressures:

> There are days when I love it but sometimes I feel sorry for myself. It's easier that I'm 45 rather than 65 – I'd hate to be taking on this responsibility at the age of 65.

In fact, nearly all the grandparents interviewed admitted that just a day of caring for a child left them exhausted. One spoke of a change in the relationship with her grandchild when – as a new full-time carer - she had to assume responsibility for discipline. For most grandparents looking after grandchildren one or two days a week that responsibility is probably taken for granted. It goes with the territory. Of course, we'd prefer to always be the archetypal loving 'Granpa and Granma' (who wouldn't?) but there are times when you're forced to take a harder line (and, in my case, I know I'd have my daughter's backing). However, if you're talking about being a full-time carer – or to use the official term, kinship carer, then the relationship with the child is going to change: you are taking on the role of parent rather than grandparent, and discipline isn't an occasional obligation, it's an on-going one.

Self-evidently, there's a sliding scale of difficulty for kinship carers. At one end, you might have the relatively young grand-parenting couple with no financial worries and one grandchild; at the other, an elderly single grandparent beset by financial problems, with more than one child to care for.

At present, there are 200,000 family carers in Britain, half of whom are grandparents, bringing up 300,000 children. Some of them are struggling – blog sites provide dramatic evidence of this. I think potential carers need to be aware of the problems but I don't want to sound negative and discouraging: there are several agencies that can really help kinship carers.

Where can kinship carers go for help?

Initially, a great deal of hands-on advice and information is available from your local Citizens Advice Bureau, but there are also websites that can put you in touch with local kinship carers and give you practical advice on a range of financial, legal, and employment issues. In particular, I'd recommend Grandparents Plus: www.grandparentsplus.org.uk. This organisation which is a national charity and Lottery funded, focuses exclusively on kinship carers. You can download or send off for their booklets/fact sheets on such topics as: the problems facing older grandparents raising their grandchildren; dealing with children's services and the legal system; managing your finances; and negotiating flexible working arrangements with your employers. They are also able to put you in touch with local kinship carer support groups.

Grandparents Plus runs the Grandparents Raising Grandchildren Network which provides vital support for kinship carers who receive little financial support as they struggle with stress, isolation and poverty. What makes matters worse is that those carers are often 'afraid to ask for help for fear of losing the children they love'.

In June 2012, Grandparents Plus produced a report based on a survey of 1,800 members of Grandparents Raising Grandchildren network. The respondents were quizzed on the kind of problems they'd experienced with employment and welfare agencies. The findings of the report make salutary reading.

Many children living in kinship care have suffered multiple traumas as a result of previously being cared for in local authority care homes (or by biological parents incapable of looking after their children). Recent cases of sexual grooming of children in Rochdale and other northern towns have highlighted the deficiencies of local authority care.

As the Grandparents Plus report points out, there's 'a strong economic case for supporting kinship carers to avoid children unnecessarily being taken into care'. It costs £40,000 per annum to keep a child in independent foster care and, in Rochdale, the cost to the local authority for the solitary 15 year-old girl repeatedly raped while in a privately run care home, was over £250,000 a year.

Given the costs involved, and the problems experienced by some children in foster care or local authority homes, you'd think cash-strapped government agencies would be falling over themselves to help kinship carers, either with grants or by leaning on employers to make special arrangements for those who need to work to fund the care of their grandchildren. Unfortunately this is not always the case.

A survey of older kinship carers found that several were struggling financially, and either unaware of grants available to them, or too proud to claim them. A clear majority 'felt deeply unhappy' with the support they had received (or not received) from children's services. 'Generally grandparents found the experience of applying for legal orders to secure their grandchildren's living arrangements stressful and expensive if they were not entitled to Legal Aid.' (*Too old to care: The experiences of older grandparents raising their grandchildren* p4)

Most carers can receive Child Benefit and Child Tax Credit and - if a child has a disability, health problems, or behavioural/emotional problems - they may be able to claim additional benefits particularly if they're on a low income. Sometimes, though, carers aren't aware of these benefits; one of the recommendations in the *Too old to care* report calls for local authorities to 'fully implement the statutory guidance on family and friends care', ensuring that carers can access financial, legal, and practical support, counselling and support groups.

Where most problems seem to occur is with employment. Kinship carers are put under pressure by social workers to give up their jobs or risk their grandchildren being taken into care or adopted.

Take the case of Donna who was a sales representative, earning £73,000 a year. She was looking after her 5 year-old grandchild, Lara, on the weekends. When her parents' relationship deteriorated, Lara came to live with her grandmother. Children's services told Lara's mother if she didn't sort out her problems, her daughter would be put up for adoption. Donna remained unaware of this threat until a solicitor friend warned of the danger. Meanwhile Donna's employer, a woman in her 60s, asked why she wasn't 'getting her granddaughter adopted'.

Donna's problems multiplied: she started using holiday leave to attend children's services and court appointments, and then took unpaid leave when her employer became increasingly unhappy with the situation. After coming under pressure from her social worker, she was forced to give up her job, because she feared Lara would be put up for adoption if she didn't. As a result, 'Donna is now dependent on benefits and at risk of losing her home'(*Giving up the day job?* P11).

Plans currently being considered by the coalition government may help women in Donna's position. Every employee will be entitled to ask their employer for the right to work flexitime. This would make it easier for grandparents to juggle work commitments and childcare. Unfortunately such a plan couldn't be introduced before 2014 at the earliest.

> Clearly, I'm not qualified to give specialised advice to kinship carers. I've simply attempted to highlight potential problems and indicate where grandparents who are raising grandchildren can go for help. Organisations like Grandparents Plus, The Grandparents' Association (www.grandparents-association.org.uk) the Family Rights group (www.frg.org.uk), Grannynet (www.grannynet.co.uk), and Citizens Advice Bureau (www.citizensadvice.org.uk) are doing a great job in both raising the profile of kinship carers, and lobbying and campaigning on their behalf. And, if you're a grandparent but not a kinship carer, you'll still find these websites are a valuable source of information on a range of issues relevant to all grandparents.

CONCLUSION

Things A Good Grandparent Should Never Forget!

Grandparents need to be seen as allies... (p.76)
'Remember Grandad... no grassing us up – OK?'

Communicating with your grandchildren is essential; communicating with their parents is equally important. With parents the 1st rule is:

- NEVER criticise the way they handle their kids – not directly anyway – unless you want to start World War 3! Even indirect criticism is best avoided. It's amazing how sensitive parents' radar is: they'll spot criticism a mile off. GO THERE AT YOUR PERIL. Remember how you resented the merest whiff of criticism (however kindly intentioned) from your own parents, or your in-laws?

The 2nd rule (jockeying for pole position with the 1st) is:

- NEVER criticise your grandchildren when talking to their parents; always find things to praise. The only exception to this rule is when a child's action has either endangered him/her self, or other children. Then you have a duty of care to inform parents. However, if it's just typical childish misbehaviour, you owe it to the child to stay sh-um. Grandparents need to be seen as allies: exchange conspiratorial nods and winks with the kids, and earn a few Brownie points.

Like any child carer, you must talk to parents about their ground rules, and their expectations of your role. At this stage, keep to yourself any reservations you might have about their rules. Later, it might be possible to say something like 'Have you ever thought about ...' or 'I wondered if you'd mind if I/we did X?' They'll probably have no objection to you doing things slightly differently from them. Our kids told us they expected us to be a little more lenient than they were; to spoil our grandchildren occasionally.

One of the perks of being a grandparent is you get to spoil your grandchildren, paint pictures and play with them, read them stories, and - at the end of an exhausting but rewarding day – hand them back to their parents, go home, put your feet up, and crack open a nice bottle of wine. (Of course it doesn't always happen quite like that)

After discussing and negotiating guidelines for kids, there may still be areas where parents and grandparents don't see eye to eye. Then I think you're entitled to say to kids, 'These are Grandpa's and Grandma's rules ...' - as long as they aren't completely at variance with what their parents regard as non-negotiable rules. If, for example, children climb over sofas and chairs in their home, I can't imagine there'd be any objections to your saying, 'No, we're sorry, we don't allow that here.'

Generally, consistency is desirable; but kids are very adaptable. They quickly learn, for example, that different codes of behaviour (and speech) apply in school, and at home. To sum up: you need the freedom to set your own boundaries, and the wisdom to know when to adjust those boundaries. At the same time, you must be sensitive to parents' wishes, and discuss things with them.

'Can't buy me love'

The desire to spoil your grandchildren occasionally, to indulge them, is natural and - up to a point – it's fine. There are things, however, you should bear in mind:

- Whenever possible, consult parents first. Of course, if you're out on a trip and want to buy your grandchild(ren) an ice-cream or a ride on a funfair, parents are unlikely to object. But if grandad sees an AK -47 toy gun and thinks, 'Just the thing for my grandson' – that's another matter. Many parents might be alarmed by the prospect of their child running around, brandishing a toy Kalishnikov and screaming, 'You're dead!' Amazingly, you can actually buy this toy gun on Amazon with an accompanying comment: 'It was great, my grandson loved it.'

- Are you better off than the parents? Regardless of your or their financial circumstances, it's not a good idea to shower presents on your grandchildren. It smacks of buying affection – rather than earning it. And it creates expectations that could become a burden later on.

- It can also be upsetting to parents: not being able to afford treats and presents could make them feel inadequate, that somehow they're letting their children down. And it's not just parents' feelings you have to think about – what about the other grandparents? Are they less well-off than you? How would you feel if you thought your grandchild's love was somehow up for sale to the highest bidder? Of course, the occasional treat or present is unlikely to provoke such extreme reactions but, once again, you need to be sensitive, and aware of how others may respond to your generosity.

- On the other hand, helping out with the essential needs of children, is altogether different. As a young family, reliant on a single income, and struggling with a mortgage, my wife and I still remember how grateful we were to our mothers for buying our children clothes and new shoes. We sometimes wonder how we would have got by without them.

- When there's more than one set of grandchildren, the question of fairness comes into play. You don't want to be seen privileging one grandchild over another. This can involve some delicate calculations! If it's one picture book for this grandchild, does it have to be the same one for the others?

You get a warm glow from treating your grandchildren. It's like treating yourself but just remember: You can't buy love; it has to be earned.

Don't be too hard on yourself!

Self criticism comes with the territory. Chances are, you were always acutely conscious of mistakes you made as a parent; as grandparents the same old doubts creep into your mind. Banish them – stop beating yourself up. You're doing a grand job. I bet the kids rush towards you when you arrive, wrap arms and legs round you and give you big hugs and kisses. Okay, if they cower in a corner and scream, you've got real problems!

Of course, there will be times when you get things wrong, feel you could have handled a particular situation differently, but sometimes there is no right way, no ideal solution. The main thing is that your grandchildren know your love is guaranteed, a comfort blanket that's always available.

And however often you wish you'd done this or that differently, your grandchildren's parents will be grateful for your help. You are, after all, an invaluable part of the child and the family's support system. Many grandparents offer financial assistance but even if they don't, they still make it possible for mothers (or fathers if there's been a role reversal) to return to the workplace. By looking after their grandchildren, grandparents are often able to reduce the cost of expensive childcare. They make a vital contribution to the family's economic independence, and beyond this, to the nation's financial well-being.

'The Devil makes work for idle hands'?

In chapter 5, I argued that many children today were being over-stimulated and that perhaps a bit of boredom was no bad thing. Boredom, I suggested, can be a source of creativity. At the time I thought I was going out on a limb. Surely such an idea would prove highly controversial and provoke derision.

Then – as this book was about to go to press – I received unexpected support. Speaking ahead of a conference on childhood at Winchester, the eminent neuroscientist and Oxford University professor, Baroness Greenfield said 'Boredom is good for children because it encourages them to be creative and develops their imaginations ... . Bored children were more likely to pick up a book or write a story, rather than being tempted to go online ... nowadays there's a tendency [to think] things have to come from outside, you have to stimulate incessantly' (Daily Mail 27th Oct 2012).

She was supported by Ed Elliott, headmaster of the Perse School, Cambridge who claimed that some youngsters have such hectic after-school diaries they are no longer allowed to think for themselves. 'Boredom', he added, 'encourages creativity. Children's bedrooms littered with bears receiving emergency treatment or dolls circumnavigating the turbulent "carpet seas" are everyday evidence of how boredom fires the imagination'.

Tributes to the potential benefits of boredom, however, seem to fly in the face of popular wisdom. As the Mail was quick to point out, Baroness Greenfield's stance was at odds with the views of many parents who believed that 'the devil makes work for idle hands' and that boredom often led to mischief. Most class teachers would agree - if children get bored they become disruptive or badly behaved.

Given my previous comments, you'd expect me to be firmly on the side of Baroness Greenfield – and I am. But with important reservations:

- as an ex-teacher I know you must keep a class of 24 (and over) pupils busily engaged in meaningful and interesting activities or they will become disruptive. Just one grandchild is a different matter.

- you can't suddenly go from a highly structured day with non-stop stimulating activities to one where periods of 'down time' are provided and children are left to their own devices. You need to gradually acclimatise them to a new regime. Growing up in the aftermath of WW2, with a much older brother, I became accustomed to boredom. Money was tight, there were no gym clubs or ballet classes, and television was in its infancy, so you were forced to make your own entertainment. Did I become more creative? I'd like to think so.

- As with most things it's a question of balance. No-one would advocate leaving children/grandchildren to play on their own (or in a completely unstructured way) for hours.

I would advise you to keep your grandchildren involved and interested **– but still allow periods of 'down time'**. Play games with them, sing with them, tell them stories, and encourage creative activities like colouring and craft work. Every grandad can join in with colouring and drawing – even if he's not very good. I'm lucky; I always enjoyed art at school but I never felt inspired when it came to Blue Peter-like 'makes'. I've often thought: if only Tony Hart (or Rolf Harris) had been around when I was young, I might have ended up a 'craftier' grandad. The less confident you are about something, the more you tend to shy away from it.

Now I've found the answer to my craft work insecurities: Usborne's *50 Rainy Day Activities*. Usborne specialises in children's books and – like all their books – this one is beautifully presented and organised. It has a range of practical ideas for 'makes' that look attractive, and children, and nervous craft-makers like me, are taken step-by-step through the different stages of making, for example, a flower bracelet, a giraffe collage, or an octopus mobile! I even felt encouraged to adapt and 'improve' some of the ideas when I tried them out on my grandchildren.

'Make us laugh, make us laugh …'

Looking after young children – especially when you're in your 70s or 80s – can be hard work. The physical and emotional pressures are sometimes underestimated. But there are always the compensations. Grandchildren bring joy into our lives – and they make us laugh. The other day a friend told me a joke. At least he said it was a joke. I like to think it was a true story:

A six-year-old came home from school and said to her grandmother, 'Grandma, guess what? We learned how to make babies today.' The grandmother, slightly alarmed and apprehensive, tried to keep her cool. 'That's interesting,' she said. 'How do you make babies?' 'It's simple,' replied the girl. 'You just change "y" to "i" and add "es".'

One final tip:

It may be stating the bleedin' obvious but it's important for you to stay fit and healthy! When young children go to playgroup or nursery school they tend to pick up colds and infections - and then pass them on to you! If you're over 65 you can get a flu jab free, and it's essential you take advantage of this protection. And if you are younger, in the 55-65 age-group, I feel it's worth paying £15 (or less) for a jab. Of course, nothing guarantees total protection but doesn't it make sense to improve your chance of avoiding illness for such a modest outlay?

That's all Folks!

Some activity rhymes to enjoy with your grandchildren:

Head shoulders, knees and toes

Head, shoulders, knees, and toes (knees and toes)
Head, shoulders, knees and toes (knees and toes)
And eyes… and ears… and mouth… and nose…
Head, shoulders, knees, and toes (knees and toes)

[touch each part of the body referred to – and I like to repeat 'knees and toes'. You can speed up with each repetition of the verse]

If you're happy and you know it, clap your hands

If you're happy and you know it, clap your hands, [clap hands twice]
If you're happy and you know it, clap your hands. [clap hands twice]
If you're happy and you know it and you really want to show it,
If you're happy and you know it, clap your hands. [clap hands twice]

If you're happy and you know it, stamp your feet. [stamp feet twice]
If you're happy and you know, it, stamp your feet, [stamp feet twice]
If you're happy and you know it and you really want to show it,
If you're happy and you know it, stamp your feet. [stamp twice]

If you're happy and you know it, shout "Hurray!" [shout "Hurray" once]
If you're happy and you know it, shout "Hurray!" [as above]
If you're happy and you know it and you really want to show it,
If you're happy and you know it, shout "Hurray!" [as above]

If you're happy and you know it do all three. [do all three!]
If you're happy and you know it do all three. [as above]

Minor variations to the above lyrics – and additional verses – can be found on line.

I'm a little teapot

I'm a little teapot,
Short and stout,
Here's my handle,   [make a 'handle with one arm in a
Here's my spout.   'D' shape and a spout with your other arm]

When I'm ready,
Hear me shout,
"Tip me up,   [tipping motion with arms as before]
And pour me out."

Incy Wincey Spider

Incy wincy spider
climbed up the water spout.

Down came the rain and . . . [raise arms and lower with fluttering
washed poor Incy out.   motion]

Out came the sun and
dried up all the rain.

And Incy wincy spider
climbed up the spout again.   [repeat climbing motion]

Some versions have 'went' up the spout rather than 'climbed'. I prefer my version but all these rhymes can be adapted and tailored to what you think sounds best.

Never smile at a crocodile

Never smile at a croc-o-dile,
'Cause you can't get friendly with a crocodile.
Don't be taken in by his friendly grin,
He's imag-i-ning how well you'd fit beneath his skin

O.K. it's not really an activity rhyme, but I love its bouncy rhythm and clever internal rhymes. It's from Disney's *Peter Pan*, and a video clip of the whole song is available on YouTube. This is the first verse but I invariably repeat it several times and it seems just the right length for my grandchildren.
[I've made a couple of very minor changes to the wording]

One, two, three, four, five

One, two, three, four, five, [hold fingers up in succession]
Once I caught a fish alive,
Six, seven, eight, nine, ten,
Then I let him go again.
Why did you let him go?
'Cos he bit my finger so.
Which finger did he bite?
This little finger on the right. [I think it's obvious what you do here]

Round and round the garden

Round and round the garden [circling motion with your finger on
Like a teddy bear tummy, then on last 2 lines take 'steps'
One step, two steps, up arm and tickle armpit]
Tickley under there!

Row, row, row your boat

Row, row, row your boat [again, with these 2 rhymes the
Gently down the stream; movements are obvious]
Merrily, merrily,
Merrily, merrily,
Life is but a dream.

Row, row your boat
Gently down the stream;
If you see a crocodile,
Don't forget to S-C-R-E-A-M!

The wheels on the bus

The wheels on the bus go round and round,
Round and round, round and round,
The wheels on the bus go round and round,
All day long

The doors on the bus go open and shut   [repeat as before]

The babies on the bus go wah, wah, wah, [repeat]

The wipers on the bus go swish, swish, swish [repeat]

The mothers on the bus go natter, natter, natter [repeat]

The fathers on the bus go snore, snore, snore [repeat]

Continue with any variations you can think of!

Zoom, zoom, zoom

Zoom, zoom, zoom,
We're going to the moon.

Zoom, zoom, zoom,
We'll be there very soon.

5, 4, 3, 2, 1,
Blast off!

If you're unfamiliar with the rhymes/songs and their accompanying actions, they can all be found online (www.bussings.com has a very comprehensive selection of lyrics, videos and suggested activities). Alternatively Usborne's First Picture Action Rhymes (with tunes on the Internet) is a beautifully presented board book with an excellent selection of rhymes.

Children's picture books: an annotated reading list

The following list makes no claims to being exhaustive: it's too short to do that. It simply represents some picture books that – over the years – have given me and my children/grandchildren particular pleasure. A sort of Desert Island library I rescued from my yacht before it sank. I've avoided giving any indication of appropriate age-range: it's often difficult correlating children's levels of maturity with their chronological age. Perhaps the best course of action is to get hold of these books yourself and make your own judgements. It's worth building up your own personal library (if a child really likes a book they will want to hear it over and over again) but if money's tight, it's worth looking in charity bookshops, or jumble sales. A very acceptable alternative is your local library – though you won't always have that favourite book to hand for re-reading. **The library is also a wonderful place to take your grandchildren.** Most have attractive sections for children with easy chairs, cushions, eye-catching book displays and exhibitions, and many organise visits from local children's writers. They are welcoming, comfy environments designed to encourage kids to catch the 'reading bug'.

Janet and Allan Ahlberg
The Jolly Postman or Other People's Letters
A postman delivers letters to the homes of fairy-tale characters like the 3 Bears, the Gingerbread Witch, and Cinderella. No child can resist opening the envelope and pulling out actual letters. The Witches envelope has a 'FREE Witch Watch with every order' message on the front and 'if undelivered return to HOBGOBLIN SUPPLIES, WARLOCK MOUNTAIN' on the back. Charming illustrations, a hilarious text which both adults and children will enjoy – utterly bewitching!

Anthony Browne
Willy the Champ
Anthony Browne (Children's Laureate 2009-11) is a children's favourite. He's fascinated by gorillas and *Gorilla* is probably his best known book. There is a series of books about Willy – a chimpanzee – but *Willy the Champ* is still my favourite. Willy's a bit of a loner – he doesn't quite fit in. He doesn't conform to macho stereotypes: he prefers books

and music to energetic sports, really likes his multi-coloured Fair Isle jumper, and is naturally a target for bullies – especially Buster Nose! Eventually (with a bit of luck) Willy triumphs over Buster. The pictures are marvellous: Buster is portrayed as a grizzled Nazi thug and Willy has an air of naive innocence. Serious issues are raised in most of Browne's books but they are always handled with humour, sensitivity, and subtlety.

John Burningham
Come Away from the Water, Shirley
Mum, Dad, and Shirley are enjoying a day trip at the seaside. On the left hand side of the page Shirley's parents read the paper, doze, tell Shirley to come away from the water, not to get dirty etc while on the right hand side, Shirley enjoys all kinds of exciting adventures and fights with Pirates. Shirley's pictures tell her story without words and the colours become increasingly vibrant. Children quickly realise two different worlds are being portrayed: the imaginative world of Shirley and the grey prosaic 'real' world of her parents. One of the joys of this book is getting children to demonstrate their visual literacy by providing a commentary/soundtrack for Shirley's adventures.

John Burningham
Granpa
See Chapter 3, pp29-30

Eric Carle
The Very Hungry Caterpillar
I'm sure this modern children's classic needs no introduction. The ideal book for toddlers and babies, it encourages interactive play: they can poke their fingers through the holes in lettuces, they can count, name foods, find out about caterpillars turning into butterflies, and enjoy the delightful pictures.

Lynley Dodd
Slinky Malinki
Ah... Slinky Malinki! A worthy successor to T.S. Eliot's 'Macavity' – except that Slinky's a mischievous cat, not a master criminal like Macavity. For me, Lynley Dodd is as good as Julia Donaldson (see below) and you can't praise more highly than that. When you've

enjoyed the *Slinky Malinki* books, there's always her *Hairy McClary* series to move on to. Dodd not only creates the marvellous pictures for her books but also the captivating rhymes. And she comes up with these memorable names – in *Slinky Malinki*, for example, we encounter the parrot, Stickybeak Syd. [Lynley Dodd is a Dame ... and there is nothing like this dame!]

Julia Donaldson – illustrated by Axel Scheffler
Room on the Broom

The current Children's Laureate is perhaps best known for *The Gruffalo*. Picking one book by Donaldson and her marvellous illustrator, Axel Scheffler, was difficult – there were so many contenders. Eventually I decided on *Room on the Broom*, a choice endorsed by my grandchildren – though *The Snail and the Whale* runs it a close second. You are probably familiar with Donaldson's hypnotic rhymes which – like Lynley Dodd's - cry out to be read aloud. What I particularly like about this tale is the incremental repetition with a succession of creatures clambering aboard the witch's broom. And, like most of the books on this list, it makes me laugh.

Debi Gliori
No Matter What
See Chapter 3, pp28-29 for a discussion of this book.

Peter Harris – illustrated by Deborah Allwright
The Night Pirates

Peter Harris and illustrator Deborah Allwright have created a book that's both a visual and an aural delight. A subtle blend of poetry and prose, and dramatic use of repetition, creates a mysterious atmosphere, which is perfectly complemented by the pictures. The story opens: They come 'down, down the street', climb up the dark, dark house, watched only by the moon, and one little boy, Tom. It's not until the 5th page that we learn they are pirates! And not just any pirates, but 'rough, tough, little girl pirates' (no gender stereotyping here). They are about to set sail on an adventure and have stolen the front of Tom's house for disguise. Tom begs to be allowed to join them and the girl captain shouts, 'Welcome aboard!'.

So, an adventure story that's not only mysterious but also surreal (and often very funny). Eventually, they reach their destination – an island where Captain Patch and his 'really rough, tough GROWN-UP pirates' are snoozing around their treasure chest. The Captain awakens to see a house approaching the shore. When it lands, Tom and the girl pirates leap out with a fearsome roar. The grown-up pirates flee, Tom and the girl pirates sail away with the treasure, and the Captain screams his 'worst pirate curse: If you don't give me my treasure back, Ill tell my MUM!'. Tom is returned with his house, it's still night-time, and in the morning the postmen scratches his head and searches for the letter box because the house is upside down!

There are lots of lovely visual details to explore, and children will find the typographical experimentation intriguing with variations in font style and size. At times you read the book horizontally, at others you turn it on end and read vertically! My grandchildren love this story and I can think of few picture books that give me greater pleasure.

Susan Hill – illustrated by Angela Barrett
Beware Beware
This atmospheric prose-poem begins with a young girl in a pinafore looking out of a kitchen window while her mother is busy at the stove. The warmth and security of the kitchen contrasts with the attraction of the world outside and the dark wood that beckons the girl. Unable to resist its lure, she slips outside and soon finds herself engulfed by the trees, within which frightening creatures lurk. Her mother arrives in the nick of time to rescue her, and the story concludes back in the warmth of the kitchen. Hill's haunting rhymes and Barrett's wonderful pictures ensure this tale exerts a powerful spell over children and adults alike. The scary scenes in the wood may make it more suitable for children in the 4-7 age range.

Shirley Hughes
All about Alfie
Distinguished author/illustrator Shirley Hughes is best known for her 'Alfie' and 'Dogger' series of books. She portrays the domestic dramas of everyday life, like Alfie accidentally locking his mother and sister out of the house, or losing his comfort blanket. Hers is a realistic yet reassuring world – one in which the disturbing perils of contemporary life are absent: children happily play in the street, and tears are soon

forgotten. A vanished world perhaps, but one conveyed with genuine warmth and affection.

Russell Hoban – illustrated by Quentin Blake
How Tom Beat Captain Najork and his Hired Sportsmen
'TOM LIVED WITH HIS MAIDEN AUNT, Miss Fidget Wonkham-Strong. She wore an iron hat and took no nonsense from anyone.' With an opening like that, who could resist this book? Russell Hoban, perhaps best known for his adult fiction (*Riddley Walker*) has also written for children (the Frances series for younger children, and *The Mouse and his Child* for older ones). Tom's a boy who loves 'fooling around'. His aunt disapproves, and tells him he should 'do something useful'. When he ignores her, she hires a nautical gentleman, Captain Najork, to cure him of 'fooling around'. The Captain engages Tom in a series of sporting challenges: the loser must submit to the other's rule. Of course, Tom's fooling around skills enable him to triumph in games like 'womble, muck, and sneedball'. The Captain marries his aunt while Tom chooses Bundlejoy Cosysweet as his new aunt. Having been outwitted by my son and daughter in most challenges (sporting or otherwise), I empathised with the Captain. Quentin Blake's illustrations perfectly complement the text.

David McKee
Not now Bernard
Bernard tries to alert his parents about the monster but they keep saying, 'Not now, Bernard'. They don't even notice that their son's been eaten by the monster – who is now masquerading as Bernard. An amusingly surreal fable for all kids who feel they're ignored by their parents. You might feel children will be scared by it: I don't think they will. *Not now Bernard* is a simple yet complex story that raises a number of issues: is the monster real or imagined? Do we ignore what children tell us - because we're too preoccupied with our own lives?

Marjorie Newman – illustrated by Kate Pankhurst
Captain Pike Looks After the Baby
Mrs Pike's busy so Captain Pike offers to take the baby with him on his next voyage. Although he's never looked after the baby, he says it'll be 'easy-peasy!' But his crew refuse to carry out the babysitting duties (like changing nappies!) he tries to foist on them, and the captain has to learn

how to feed, wind, and get the baby to sleep. Despite some hiccups, all is going well till a pirate ship is sighted, manned by their deadly enemies - Captain Whitebeard and his crew. Pandemonium ensues, and the baby wakes up and starts bawling. Fortunately, the situation is peacefully resolved: Captain Whitebeard is a family man who loves children. He stays all day to play peep-bo, and sing lullabies. The pirates discover it's much more fun being friends than fighting all the time. Illustrator, Kate Pankhurst, extracts every ounce of humour from this delightful tale.

Hiawyn Oram – illustrated by Satoshi Kitamura
Angry Arthur
'Arthur wants to watch TV but his mother won't let him. "I'll get angry," said Arthur, and he did. Very, very angry...' This picture-book has quickly established itself as a modern classic. Kitamura's ravishing illustrations complement the spare text as Arthur's anger swiftly escalates into a storm of intergalactic proportions. Most children will identify with the frustration of Arthur and it's an ideal book for discussing anger management problems. Check out the other collaborations of Oram and Kitamura – you won't be disappointed.

Michael Rosen – illustrated by Helen Oxenbury
We're Going on a Bear Hunt
I'm sure neither Michael Rosen (former Children's Laureate) nor *We're Going on a Bear Hunt* needs any introduction from me. Why are children so attracted to this book? Well, it's partly the excitement of the chase, partly the lovely onomatopoeic words like 'squelch' and 'swishy-swashy', and also the patterned repetitive sequences which children quickly learn by heart. It won't be long, in fact, before your child can recite the whole story. My grand-daughter was bewitched by the stage adaptation I took her to but seemed unimpressed when Grandpa told her he had once taught Mr Rosen. (it was on an M.A. Course, and it's probably more accurate to say Mr Rosen taught me!). This is a book that will appeal to all children and adults.

Tony Ross
I Want My Potty
Most people find this hilarious book helps with potty training; a few don't. Of course, it's not intended as a potty training manual! Children love it – and so, I bet, will you.

Maurice Sendak
Where The Wild Things Are
Max – wearing his wolf suit – has been making mischief. His mother calls him, 'WILD THING', and he's sent to bed without his supper. That night a forest grows in Max's bedroom and he sails off in his boat 'through night and day and in and out of weeks... to where the wild things are.' Despite roaring their terrible roars, gnashing their terrible teeth and showing their terrible claws, the wild things can't intimidate Max. He tames them with a magic spell, saying, 'Let the wild rumpus start!' Eventually, Max tires of the wild things, sends them to bed without their supper and returns home to find his (hot) supper waiting.

Winner of the Caldecott Medal in 1964, *Where The Wild Things Are* heralded a new golden age of picture books. Max's fantasy world not only provides an outlet for his anger, but allows him to come to terms with it. The book provoked controversy when it was first published, and was banned by some libraries. Nowadays, this profound psychological study of anger is recognised as a classic. Many early critics assumed it was too frightening for children, ignoring the book's humour, and the fact that Max completely controls the wild things (just as his mother strives to control him). Soon children clamoured to have the book read to them, and critics revised their opinion. The pictures perfectly match the text of this simple yet sophisticated tale.

Posy Simmonds
Fred
Author/illustrator Posy Simmonds, probably best known for her adult strip cartoons, Posy and Tamara Drew, has also produced a number of children's books. *Fred* follows the same strip cartoon format. Sophie and Nick are feeling sad: their cat, Fred, has just died. No, please, don't laugh - but that's just what these pictured memories of Fred make you do. It's another of those books that help children come to terms with death. Later that night, Sophie and Nick are awakened by Ginger, a neighbour's cat who invites them to a celebration of Fred's life by all the local cats. The ensuing funeral celebration is hilarious and touching.

Valerie Thomas and Korky Paul
Winnie's Midnight Dragon
If you're not familiar with Valerie Thomas', and illustrator, Korky Paul's,

Winnie the Witch series, you're in for a treat. Winnie has a cat called Wilbur who seems to cause havoc wherever he goes – especially when he starts chasing a dragon around Winnie's home. The illustrations are funny and captivating, and I love the Gothic mansion Korky Paul has created for Winnie.

Jill Tomlinson
The Owl Who Was Afraid of the Dark
See Chapter 3, p28

Susan Varley
Badger's Parting Gifts
See Chapter 3, p30

Poetry Anthologies

I was intending to confine my annotated bibliography to picture books but felt there were just a few poetry anthologies that couldn't be left behind when I ended up on my desert island. There are 100s of anthologies to choose from – and I have selected three! Clearly this is a (very) personal choice, not a comprehensive selection.

Pie Corbett and Gaby Morgan
A First Poetry Book
With over 250 poems, Corbett and Morgan's selection can claim to be pretty comprehensive. This anthology was published in 2012 and though it includes poems by some well-known children's poets, it was refreshing to come across so many excellent poems from poets who were unfamiliar to me (and, I suspect, my readers). Arranged by theme, it includes poems about: fairies; monsters, mythical creatures and dinosaurs; pets and animals; festivals; minibeasts; friends; and many other topics. All that's missing are illustrations; presumably, because to have done so would have made it a very fat book. It's still a wonderful book to have for bed-time reading to children.

Debi Gliori
Noisy Poems
In this selection, the illustrations – by Gliori - are as much a source of pleasure as the poems. For example, in Charles Causley's delightful nonsense poem'"Quack!"Said the Billy Goat', the animals have speech bubbles with the cow saying 'Cluck' and the owl saying "Bleat! Bleat!". The first poem, Spike Milligan's 'On the Ning Nang Nong' brings back happy memories of holidays in Devon: we had a tape in the car of Milligan's poems for the journey to keep the kids entertained (what really produced fits of uncontrollable giggles, however, was 'Bare Bottom Land' in Milligan's fairy story, *Bad Jelly the Witch*). As Noisy Poems suggests, these poems are great for reading aloud.

Jane Yolen and Andrew Fusek Peters – illustrations by Polly Dunbar
Here's a Little Poem
Jane Yolen dedicates this book to her grandchildren and all poetry

lovers. It's designed to appeal to a wide age range: from very young children to those aged 70 plus. Like *A First Poetry Book* it's arranged in topics: Me, Myself and I; Who Lives in My House?; I Go Outside; and Time for Bed. Looking at this large format book is like looking at a work of art with beautiful illustrations and different coloured fonts to match the dominant colour of the page background.

There are poems by such well-known poets as John Agard, Wendy Cope, Spike Milligan, Roger McGough, A.A Milne, Grace Nicholls, Michael Rosen, and R. L. Stevenson. One of my favourites, however, is 'Ivy Says' by a less well-known poet, Philip Waddell (he also has several poems in *A First Poetry Book*). The Sunday Times said, 'This lovely book deserves a place in every child's library'. Because of the artwork and size, it's more expensive than many children's poetry books but worth every penny.

Finally, one poetry book that's not an anthology – A.A. Milne's *When We Were Very Young*. Milne has been derided by some critics for his cosy, sentimental portrayal of an upper middle-class milieu. Perhaps they're right but one shouldn't lose sight of the fact that many of his poems for children are brilliant, witty, charming and verbally inventive. Take 'The Three Foxes' which is reminiscent of Milligan's inspired word-play:
    Once upon a time there were three little foxes
    Who didn't wear stockings, and they didn't wear socksies

Later we learn :
    They didn't go shopping in the High Street shopses
    But caught what they wanted in the woods and copses.
    They all went fishing and they caught three wormses,
    They went out hunting, and they caught three wopses.

I must confess there's a nostalgic element in my affection for Milne. My mother read these poems to me, I read them to my children and now I read them to my grandchildren. That's three generations that have loved them. I can still recite all of 'The King's breakfast' (you may recall the King was not a fussy man but he did like 'a little bit of butter to his bread' and – my favourite – 'Disobedience' which begins:
James James
Morrison Morrison

Weatherby George Dupree
Took great
Care of his mother,
Though he was only three.
James James
Said to his mother,
"Mother", he said, said he;
"You must never go down to the end of the town, if you don't go down with me."